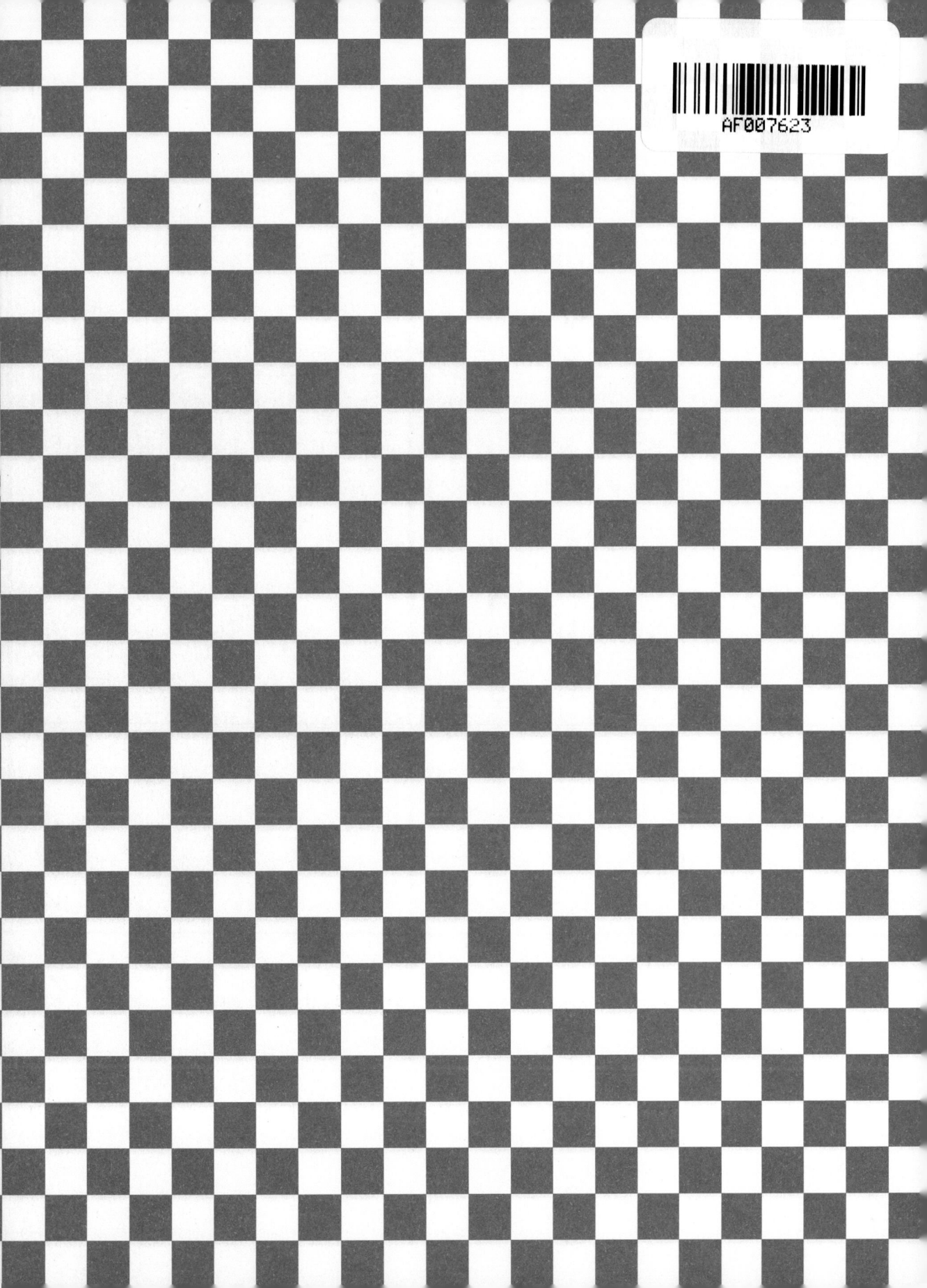

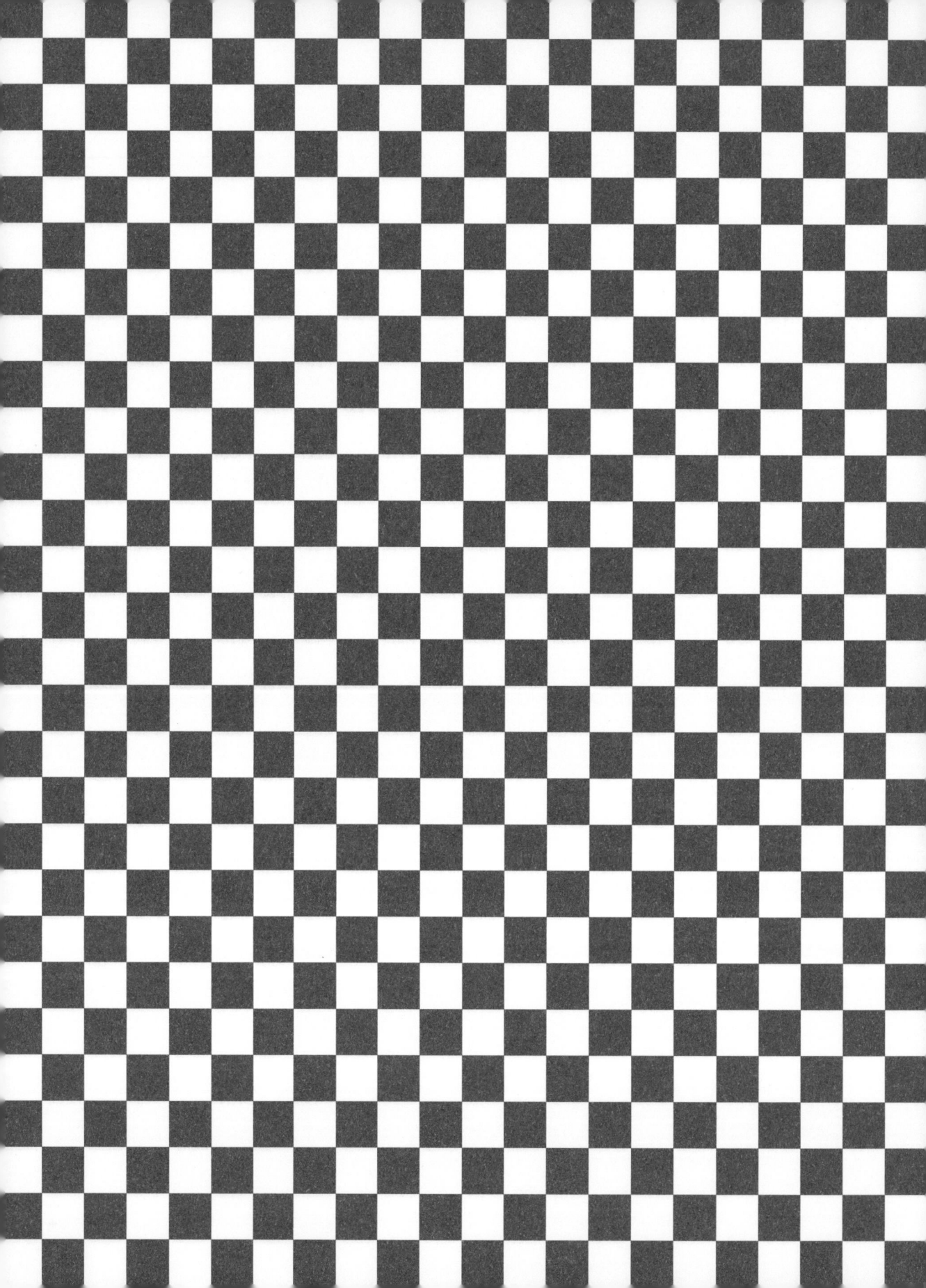

Gennaro's
HIDDEN ITALY

Gennaro's HIDDEN ITALY

REGIONAL RECIPES TO TREASURE FOR GENERATIONS

PAVILION

CONTENTS

Introduction 6

CENTRAL ITALY
14

Fresh Ring Pasta With Vegetables And Ricotta	20
Chitarra Pasta With Lamb Ragù	24
Handmade Pasta With Beans	28
Pope's Pasta Dish	30
Frascarelli With Vegetable Ragù	32
Handmade Pasta In A Broth Of Greens And Tomato	34
Medieval Pancakes	38
Savoury Spelt Bake	40
Cicoria Soup With Cheese And Eggs	42
Tuna And Pickle Pie	44
Octopus Pie	45
Polenta Dumplings With Sausage And Broccoli	48
Roast Pork Shank With Apicius Sauce	50
Three-Meat Stew	52
Ricotta And Cherry Tart	54
Almond And Chocolate Loaf Cake	56
Almond Biscuits	58
Honey And Walnut Pastry Roll	59
Chickpea And Chocolate Pastries	60
Chestnut Puddings	62

ISLANDS
64

Pasta With Anchovies And Breadcrumbs	72
Busiate Pasta With Trapani Pesto	74
Lorighittas Pasta With Seafood	78
Sardinian Malloreddus Pasta With Sausage And Creamy Pecorino	82
Sardinian Couscous With Vegetables	84
Polenta Soup	85
Cheesy Potato Fritters	88
Seafood Cousous	90
Filled Baked Sardines	94
Ischia-Style Rabbit	98
Stuffed Beef Pot Roast	99
Stuffed And Boiled Chicken	102
Sardinian Bread Rolls Filled With Potato, Cheese And Mint	104
Aniseed Bread	106
Sardinian Bread Bake With Tomato And Poached Eggs	108
Flower-Shaped Ricotta-Filled Pastries	110
Watermelon Jelly	112
Custard-Filled Pastries	114
Honey Pie	116
Almond-Filled Pastries	118

Vegetarian   Vegan   Egg-free   Gluten-free

NORTH
120

SOUTH
168

Baked Tagliolini Pasta	*130*
Pasta Pie	*131*
Baked Venetian-Style Gnocchi	*134*
Walnut Lasagne	*136*
Sweet And Savoury Ravioli	*138*
Courgettes With Amaretti	*140*
Cheesy Cabbage Bake	*141*
Creamy Salt Cod	*142*
Trout Fillets With Anchovy Sauce	*144*
Slow-Cooked Beef	*146*
Sweet And Sour Chicken Liver Sauce	*147*
Semolina Cubes In Meat Broth	*148*
Mini Milanese Fritto Misto	*150*
Bean And Sausage Risotto	*152*
Pork Rolls	*154*
Rice Bread Rolls	*155*
Filled Brioche	*158*
Sponge, Hazelnut Cream And Marzipan Cake	*160*
Sweet Polenta Fritters	*163*
Fruit And Honey Cake	*164*

Assassin's Spaghetti	*176*
Handmade Long Pasta with Chickpeas And Dried Peppers	*178*
Roasted Lampascioni And Potatoes	*182*
Green Peppers With Scrambled Eggs	*184*
Calabrian Fileja Pasta With 'Nduja And Sweet Tropea Onions	*185*
Lenten 'Meatballs'	*186*
Stewed Squid And Potatoes	*188*
Soup of Cicerchie	*192*
Meatballs 'Street Food Style'	*194*
Mutton Stew From Molise	*198*
Neapolitan Pork And Cabbage Soup	*199*
Stuffed Baked Tromboncino	*200*
Potato-Base Pizza	*202*
Savoury Fried Dough Balls	*203*
Tomato And Anchovy Bread	*204*
Fisherman's Loaf	*206*
Carnival Pastries With Chocolate Dip	*208*
Almond Biscuits	*212*
Cherry And Custard Brioche Cake	*214*
Sweet Treats from Galatina	*218*

Index *220*
Acknowledgements *224*

INTRODUCTION

Purists will say that an Italian cuisine does not exist and that dishes should always be classified as Piemontese, Veneziana, Romana, Napoletana, Sarda and so on, because all 20 of Italy's regions have such a distinct culture of their own. In fact, the country only became unified in 1861 and, until then, was made up of separate city-states and regions, each defined by their own rich histories and traditions, and especially by their food culture. There is an Italian term that expresses this exactly – *campanilismo* – which refers to the *campanile* (bell tower) that is central to every town and village and symbolically represents the identity of the locale. Even today, Italians take a lot of pride in defending their local identity, especially on the islands and in smaller villages, and this is very much reflected in the continuity of individual traditions. When it comes to food, not only is a regional speciality particular to each town, but often the recipe is particular to each family. Everyone has their own version, which they claim is the only correct one!

Food in Italy remained very regional up until the Second World War, after which people began to travel more. Southern Italians headed north to find work opportunities and the affluent travelled to different regions on holiday. With this movement of people, ingredients also began to travel. The northern staple risotto, for example, became embraced in the South, where they combined it with local produce to create new recipes. And of course nowadays, with TV, books and social media, recipes are shared globally and food that is distinct and unique to a region is almost a thing of the past. However, in Italy there are still many products that are produced and consumed almost exclusively within a certain territory and that's what makes Italy's food culture so unique.

In my lifetime, food trends have undergone huge changes in Italy as everyone adapts to the fast pace of modern life. In larger cities, time constraints don't permit long three-course lunches, and certain dishes, which I remember well from my childhood, are rarely eaten, if at all. When I was young, I would dip day-old bread into milky coffee for breakfast, but this tradition has long disappeared in favour of patisserie-style brioche and croissants. I also remember a quick morning pick-me-up made with egg yolks, beaten with sugar and coffee, which my mother would insist I have for extra energy throughout the day – but this has also fallen out of fashion as I think people are now afraid of consuming raw eggs. The typical kids' teatime snack of *pane, burro e marmelata* (bread, butter and jam) is no longer a popular choice among youngsters. And my childhood treat of pig's blood with chocolate or carob is not something kids would eat these days, unless perhaps in rural communities. And light evening meals like *Riso e Latte* or *Polenta e Latte* (rice or polenta with milk) are no longer served, except perhaps for the older generation.

For me, Italy is an emotion – the wonderful historic cities, quaint villages lost in time, landscapes, traditions, the people and of course the food. When I visit, I like to go off the beaten track, explore the lesser-known towns and villages, seek out the family-run *trattorie*, the ones without written menus. And, if I'm lucky, I'll find a *sagra* (festival) where food products are celebrated and traditions kept alive. Because despite the inevitable changes modern life brings with it, food culture is so ingrained in the Italian psyche that regional identity always shines through. You can introduce a thousand new cuisines in Italy but, at the end of the day, the dishes of our grandmothers and mothers are the ones we yearn for and they are just as important today as they have always been.

Introduction 11

It has taken me almost a lifetime of travelling throughout different parts of Italy to discover the amazing diversity my country has to offer. I love the contrast between the cooler north, with its rich buttery dishes, and the sun-baked south, where tomatoes and olive oil take centre stage. Influences can be traced to our French, Germanic and Slavic neighbours in the north, as well as to past Arab invasions of the islands in the South, and all have had a profound effect on Italian cuisine and further added to its diversity.

In this book, I am taking you on a culinary journey of discovery across Italy's diverse landscape of plains, mountains, rivers and lakes and to the shores of the Mediterranean and Adriatic seas, to find many wonderful recipes that have been lost in time or simply gone out of fashion, many of which can be traced to a particular town or village. I hope you will enjoy recreating these lesser-known recipes and, by doing so, you too will keep the culinary traditions of Italy alive.

CENTRAL ITALY

The regions of Tuscany, Umbria, Le Marche, Lazio and Abruzzo make up the heart of Italy. However, before the country was unified in 1861, the only two regions of central Italy were the Grand Duchy of Tuscany and the Papal State of Rome, which included the areas of Lazio, Le Marche and Umbria. Ask anyone from Tuscany and they will say that the real Italian is spoken in Florence. Ask a Roman and they will tell you that Rome is the cradle of Mediterranean cuisine.

Central Italy has a rich, farming tradition. Beans and ancient grains such as *farro* (spelt) are a common crop, lentils grow profusely and each region has its own speciality, like the highly prized Castelluccio variety from Umbria or *Lenticchie di Santo Stefano di Sessanio* from the Gran Sasso National Park in Abruzzo. All these ingredients feature in the hearty soups and pasta dishes that the region is famous for and, in general, the local food traditions are simple but hearty and robust, designed primarily to feed hardworking labourers in the fields.

Summers are hot in Central Italy and so tomato-based dishes and olive oil are used more than in the North. However, inland, the winters are cold, making it possible to grow leafy vegetables like cavolo nero. On the hilly and mountainous hinterland terrain, chestnut trees abound and, in the past, the nuts were often ground and made into flour for all sorts of sweet and savoury dishes. These days, chestnut flour is not so commonly used, except for local specialities like the sweet Tuscan *Castagnaccio* cake, and chestnuts are roasted and eaten or added to dishes whole.

The quality of Tuscan food is renowned worldwide, especially its olive oil and wine, as well as the large white Chianina cattle used to make the classic Italian steak dish *Bistecca alla Fiorentina*. The Etruscans, who predated the Ancient Romans, occupied the territory known today as Tuscany. Food was a very important part of Etruscan culture and they found the land ideal for growing produce like olives, grains, beans and pulses, foraging for truffles and hunting wild boar. Their traditions lay the foundation for much of Tuscany's great and varied cuisine.

Umbria, the only landlocked region of Central Italy, is home to wonderful forests and is often known as *il cuore verde d'Italia* (the green heart of Italy). Wild porcini mushrooms and truffles can be found in the woods and these ingredients flavour many local dishes. The food of the region is rich with meat and game, and shavings of truffle piled high over pasta are the norm in local restaurants. Cured meats are a speciality, particularly in Norcia where wild boar hunting provides plentiful sausages, hams and salami, which are all on display in the mouth-watering delis of every town.

While beef rules in Tuscany, lamb is king in Lazio and Abruzzo, where *abbacchio* (baby milk-fed lamb) is a speciality at Eastertime in Rome and *Agnello Cacio e Ova* (lamb in an egg and cheese sauce) in Abruzzo. Not forgetting barbecued *Scotaditto* and *Arrosticini* for a finger-licking treat.

In comparison to Tuscany and Lazio, the regions of Le Marche and Abruzzo were historically poor regions. As in the North, polenta is a staple of the diet, along with simple pastas made with flour and water. However, fish from the coast, shepherd dishes from the mountains and vegetables from the hills also feature in the cuisine of both regions, and cured pork products and local cheeses are plentiful too. Abruzzo prides itself on the cultivation of saffron near the region's capital of L'Aquila, as well as a unique garlic from Sulmona with small bulbs and deliciously sweet cloves.

The region of Lazio centres itself on the cuisine of Rome. Everything about Rome is *la dolce vita,* where food is plentiful and life is laid-back and to be enjoyed, and these traditions contain echoes of ancient times, when banquets were a gastronomic feast, also featuring the favoured Roman produce of cheese, lamb, olives and fresh vegetables. And these days, Roman food is also identified with many iconic pasta dishes – *Carbonara, Amatriciana, Cacio e Pepe* and *Pasta alla Gricia* with its strong flavours of *guanciale* (cured pork cheek) and Pecorino cheese.

Central Italy 17

Although offal may be on the decline, Rome still has a strong tradition of using the lesser cuts and innards, known as the *quinto quarto*, meaning fifth quarter. This term dates back centuries to when, in the slaughterhouses of the Testaccio neighbourhood in Rome, the best quarter of the butchered animal was reserved for the nobles, the second quarter for the clergy, the third for the bourgeois, the fourth for the army, and the fifth (organ meat) went to the poor. The brains, heart, lungs, feet and intestines went into the cooking pot and, in classic *cucina povera*-style, created some of Rome's most famous dishes, like *Coda alla Vaccinara* (oxtail stew) or *Coratella d'Agnello* (pluck of lamb) or *Pajata* (intestines of a baby calf or lamb). These dishes may not be made at home these days, but they are still on the menu in many of the city's restaurants and eateries.

Wonderful fresh artichokes are also a speciality of Rome and in season can be found in the city's markets, sitting in buckets of acidulated water, ready-prepared to take home and cook. The local Jewish-inspired dish of *Carciofi alla Giudea,* in which they are served crispy and fried, is very popular and can be found in the many restaurants of the city's Jewish Quarter.

Historically, Jews have lived in Tuscany and Rome for millennia, many fleeing from Spain towards the end of the 1400s and welcomed in the Papal state until banished to the ghetto in the mid-1500s. Hailing from the Iberian Peninsula, Sephardic Jewish cuisine integrated well with Mediterranean ingredients and diet. *Baccalà* (salt cod), for example, gradually became popular in Rome and when, in 1661, the Papal government banned ghetto residents from eating 'luxury' foods, such as large fish, the Jews began to create broths and pasta dishes using anchovies and sardines. Cheesecakes made with Italian ricotta were made in Jewish bakeries, as well as a variety of desserts with nuts and honey. These specialities are still being made in traditional delis and restaurants in the Jewish Quarter in Rome.

From thick Chianina beef steaks, served with some of the world's best red wines, to rustic *cucina povera* dishes of beans and pulses, the dishes of the central regions of Italy really are a wonderful eclectic mix and I hope this chapter will be full of fresh discoveries for you.

ANELLINI ALLA PECORARA

Fresh ring pasta with vegetables and ricotta

This traditional Abruzzese recipe comes from the rural area of Elice, where sheep dominated the land. Shepherds' wives would make this laborious but wonderful fresh pasta with a sauce of vegetables and sheep's cheese and, while it is still made in the area today, it is usually reserved for special occasions. If you can, use sheep's ricotta for maximum flavour and, if you don't have time to make fresh *anellini*, simply use a short pasta shape like farfalle or conchiglie to go with the delicious creamy sauce.

SERVES 4

For the dough
150 g/5½ oz 00 flour
150 g/5½ oz durum wheat semolina flour (semola rimacinata), plus extra for dusting
3 eggs, lightly beaten
75 ml/2½ fl oz extra virgin olive oil
approx. 1 tbsp water

For the sauce
4 tbsp extra virgin olive oil
½ small onion, finely chopped
¼ celery stalk, finely chopped
½ small carrot, finely chopped
350 g/12 oz baby plum tomatoes, cut in half
2 garlic cloves, crushed and left whole
½ small red pepper, deseeded and diced
½ small yellow pepper, deseeded and diced
½ large aubergine, diced
½ small courgette, diced
150 g/5½ oz ricotta, well-drained
30 g/1 oz grated Pecorino cheese, plus extra to serve
sea salt and freshly ground black pepper

Recipe continues overleaf

First make the pasta dough. In a bowl or stand mixer, combine the flours, then gradually add the beaten eggs and olive oil with about 1 tablespoon of water to make a smooth dough. Roll into a ball, cover with clingfilm or a cloth, and set aside to rest while you prepare the sauce.

In a pan, heat 2 tablespoons of olive oil and sweat the onion, celery and carrot over a medium heat for about 2 minutes. Add the tomatoes with a little salt, cover with a lid, and cook over a medium heat for about 20 minutes, until the tomatoes have softened.

In another pan, heat the remaining olive oil and sweat the garlic cloves over a medium heat for a minute or so to infuse the oil. Discard the garlic cloves, then stir-fry the peppers for 5–6 minutes until softened but not mushy. Remove and set aside.

In the same pan, stir-fry the aubergine for about 4 minutes until cooked, then remove and set aside. Stir-fry the courgette in the pan for about 3 minutes, until softened but not mushy, then remove and set aside.

In a bowl, combine the ricotta and Pecorino with a little black pepper. Add the tomato mixture and all the stir-fried vegetables and gently mix together. Set aside.

Take small pieces of the dough (approx. 50g/1¾ oz) and roll into very long snake-like shapes, as thin as you can. Wrap around your index finger, then cut and pinch the ends together to form a ring shape. Place the rings on a lightly floured board and cover with clingfilm or a cloth to avoid the pasta drying out while you make the rest.

Bring a large pot of salted water to the boil and cook the *anellini* for 12–15 minutes. Meanwhile, place the vegetable and ricotta mixture into a large frying pan and gently heat through.

When the pasta is cooked, use a spider utensil or slotted spoon to transfer it to the pan with the sauce. Mix well together and cook over a medium heat for about a minute.

Serve immediately with an extra sprinkling of grated Pecorino and black pepper.

CHITARRA CON RAGÙ DI AGNELLO

Chitarra pasta with lamb ragù

This dish is a speciality from the mountainous Abruzzo region. The combination of handmade pasta, flavoured with local saffron and succulent lamb is a winner.

SERVES 4–6

For the pasta dough

400 g/14 oz durum wheat semolina flour (semola rimacinata), plus extra for dusting

pinch of sea salt

4 eggs, lightly beaten

4 strands of saffron, diluted in a little lukewarm water

For the ragù

2 tbsp extra virgin olive oil

1 small onion, finely chopped

350 g/12 oz minced lamb

2 medium-sized porcini mushrooms, finely chopped

2½ tbsp white wine

400 ml/14 fl oz hot vegetable stock

5 small saffron strands, diluted in the vegetable stock

small bunch of herbs (rosemary, thyme and sage), tied together

grated Pecorino cheese, to serve

sea salt and freshly ground black pepper

First make the pasta dough. Place the flour and salt in a bowl, make a well in the centre, add the beaten eggs and saffron water and mix well to form a soft dough. Cover with clingfilm or a cloth and set aside in the fridge to rest for 30 minutes.

In the meantime, make the ragù. Place the olive oil in a pan over a medium heat and sweat the onion for a couple of minutes to soften. Add the minced lamb and brown well all over, then stir in the porcini mushrooms. Increase the heat, add the white wine and allow to evaporate, then add the stock with the saffron strands, the herbs and a little salt and pepper to season. Cover with a lid and gently cook for 50–60 minutes until nearly all the liquid has been absorbed.

On a lightly floured surface, roll out the dough to about 5 mm/¼ inch thick – or use the no. 2 setting on a pasta machine. Cut a rectangular piece of dough, place over the *chitarra* and, with a rolling pin, press down over the dough until it slices into spaghetti-type strands. Transfer these to a lightly floured board, cover with clingfilm or a cloth to avoid drying out and continue rolling the remaining pasta over the *chitarra*.

Bring a large pot of salted water to the boil and cook the *chitarra* pasta for about 3 minutes until 'al dente'. When cooked, use tongs to transfer the pasta to the lamb ragù, adding a little of the pasta water if necessary, and mix well over a high heat for about a minute.

Serve immediately with a sprinkling of grated Pecorino.

Ingredient Note

To make the *chitarra* pasta, you need a tool known as a *chitarra* (guitar), which is easily obtainable online. This ancient tool has a rectangular wooden frame with thin guitar-like strings running lengthways, which cut the dough shape. However, you can also use ready-made spaghetti instead.

26 Central Italy

Central Italy

CAZZARIELLI CON FAGIOLI (CASSARJELLE E FASCJULE)

Handmade pasta with beans

This hearty and nutritious dish falls somewhere between a soup and a pasta – perfect for the cooler months. I had the pleasure of tasting it at an autumn food festival in the Abruzzo region showcasing the area's typical produce. The beans were a local black and white variety and the pasta flour was locally milled. For extra flavour, I have added pancetta and a little chilli but these can be omitted if you prefer.

SERVES 4

For the pasta

400 g/14 oz 00 flour, plus extra for dusting

200 ml/7 fl oz lukewarm water

For the sauce

4 tbsp extra virgin olive oil, plus extra for drizzling

60 g/2¼ oz pancetta, finely chopped

4 garlic cloves, crushed and left whole

½ red chilli, finely chopped (optional)

2 small sprigs of rosemary

4 tbsp tomato passata

2 x 400 g/14 oz tins of borlotti beans

approx. 200 ml/7 fl oz hot vegetable stock

20 g/¾ oz grated Parmesan cheese

First make the pasta dough. Place the flour in a large bowl or on a clean work surface, make a well in the centre and gradually add 200 ml/7 fl oz lukewarm water, mixing to make a soft dough. Knead lightly until smooth, then wrap in clingfilm and rest for 20 minutes. Alternatively, you can use a stand mixer.

Take a small piece of dough (approx. 100g/3½ oz – keeping the rest covered to avoid drying out) and roll into a long thin sausage shape (approx. 5 mm/¼ inch in diameter), then cut into approx. 5 mm/¼ inch lengths. Place the *cazzarielli* onto a lightly floured board and cover with a cloth while you repeat with the remaining dough.

To make the sauce, heat the olive oil in a large, deep-sided frying pan and sweat the pancetta for a couple of minutes. Add the garlic, chilli and rosemary and sweat for another minute or so. Stir in the passata and borlotti beans with their liquid, along with the vegetable stock. Bring to the boil, then reduce the heat and gently cook for 8–10 minutes, until reduced and thickened.

In the meantime, bring a large pot of salted water to the boil, drop in the *cazzarielli* and cook for about 8 minutes until softened. When the pasta is cooked, use a spider utensil to transfer it to the beans. Mix well, along with a little of the pasta water, and cook for another couple of minutes. Stir in the grated Parmesan and drizzle with a little extra virgin olive oil, which will give it a nice creamy consistency, then serve immediately.

Ingredient Note

This Abruzzese pasta, known as *cazzarielli*, really makes this dish. It is an easy one to make, from just flour and water, and is cut into small gnocchi-type shapes.

FETTUCCINE ALLA PAPALINA

Pope's pasta dish

The story behind this pasta dish dates back to the 1930s, when Cardinal Pacelli, who later became Pope Pius XII, asked a restaurant near the Vatican in Rome to make him a lighter version of the classic Spaghetti alla Carbonara. So, the chef replaced durum wheat semolina spaghetti with homemade egg fettucine, used cooked ham in place of guanciale and Parmesan instead of the stronger-tasting Pecorino. Some sources suggest cream was used in place of the egg yolks, but it is unclear when peas were added. But whatever the story, it's another fantastic example of Roman cuisine and it makes a wonderful quick and simple main course at any time.

SERVES 4

1 tbsp extra virgin olive oil
50 g/1¾ oz butter
1 large onion, finely chopped
120 g/4¼ oz frozen peas
200 g/7 oz cooked ham, thickly cut, cut into small cubes
320 g/11½ oz egg fettuccine (or tagliatelle)
6 egg yolks
60 g/2¼ oz grated Parmesan cheese
sea salt and freshly ground black pepper

Place a pan over a gentle heat, melt the olive oil and butter and steam-fry the onion for about 10 minutes until softened.

Turn the heat up to medium, add the frozen peas and ham with a little salt and pepper and cook for about 4 minutes until the peas are cooked.

Meanwhile, bring a large pot of salted water to the boil and cook the fettuccine until 'al dente' (check the instructions on the packet for precise cooking times).

In a bowl, whisk together the egg yolks and grated Parmesan with a little black pepper.

When the pasta is cooked, drain and transfer to the pan with the peas and ham, along with a little of the pasta cooking water. Mix together and cook over a high heat for a minute, so everything is well combined.

Remove from the heat, pour in the egg mixture, mix well and serve immediately with a sprinkling of black pepper.

Ingredient Note
Ask your deli to cut the ham into a thick piece, which you can then cut into small cubes.

FRASCARELLI CON RAGÙ DI VERDURE

Frascarelli with vegetable ragù

This unusual dish from the region of Le Marche is quite ancient in origin and said to date back to the Romans. Traditionally, the *frascarelli* was piled onto a wooden board and topped with a ragù sauce, before everyone tucked in. Created from little solid flour balls, it seems like a strange dish but is especially delicious with this nourishing vegetable ragù.

SERVES 4

For the vegetable ragù
- abundant vegetable or sunflower oil, for shallow-frying
- 1 medium-sized courgette (approx. 150 g/5½ oz), cut into half-moon slices
- 1 medium-sized aubergine (approx. 140 g/5 oz), cut into small cubes
- 1 red or yellow pepper (approx. 150 g/5½ oz), sliced
- 1 small onion, finely chopped
- 2 tbsp extra virgin olive oil
- 400 ml/14 fl oz tomato passata
- 100 g/3½ oz frozen peas
- a few basil leaves
- grated Parmesan cheese, to serve
- sea salt and freshly ground black pepper

For the frascarelli
- 200 g/7 oz 00 flour
- 1 egg
- 25 ml/5 tsp water, plus a little extra
- 1 litre/1¾ pints water (for the rice)
- 25 g/1 oz arborio rice

First make the vegetable ragù. Place abundant oil in a pan over a medium-high heat and, once hot, cook the cut vegetables separately (i.e. the courgettes then the aubergines followed by the pepper), frying for 2–3 minutes until golden. Remove with a slotted spoon and drain on kitchen paper.

Discard the used vegetable oil, give the pan a quick wipe, then place back over a medium heat. Sweat the onion in the olive oil until softened, then add the tomato passata, together with a little water from rinsing out the jar or carton, and season. Cover with a lid and simmer for 5 minutes, then add the fried vegetables and cook for 10 more minutes. Add the peas and basil leaves and continue to cook for a further 5 minutes.

Now make the *frascarelli*. In a bowl, place the flour and egg with 25 ml/5 tsp water and rub together with your fingers to mix, as you would when making a crumble, to obtain tiny solid balls. Shake the mixture through a fine sieve into a bowl, then transfer the balls left in the sieve onto a flat plate or board. Sprinkle a little more over the remaining flour in the bowl and rub together to make more balls. Repeat this process until all the flour is used up, and you have lots of solid flour balls (the *frascarelli*).

In a large pan, bring 1 litre/1¾ pints salted water to the boil, add the rice and cook for about 8 minutes until nearly cooked. Drop the *frascarelli* into the boiling water with the rice, whisking well for about 8 minutes, until the mixture thickens to a polenta-type consistency. Keep tasting as you go to test if the flour is cooked – you may need a little more or less cooking time.

Pour the *frascarelli* onto a large serving dish, ladle the vegetable ragù on top and sprinkle with grated Parmesan before serving.

Ingredient Notes
Frascarelli is a *cucina povera* classic. Made simply from flour and water, no fancy machinery is required, not even a rolling pin, just your hands and a fine sieve. The addition of rice prevents the mixture from becoming a complete mush, and the trick is to whisk continuously as it cooks.

SURGI SFUNNET' CO' LE FOGLIA

Handmade pasta in a broth of greens and tomato

I first had this soup in a restaurant in Castel del Monte, overlooking the Gran Sasso National Park in Abruzzo. The pasta, made only with flour and water, is said to be in the shape of *surgi,* meaning mice in local dialect, although I can't see the resemblance. They are actually more like pea pods and there is a similar shape in Puglia known locally as *capunti.* The *surgi* finish cooking in a broth of tomatoes and *cime di rapa*, and this simple dish, using only a few local ingredients, is both warming and satisfying.

SERVES 4

400 g/14 oz 00 flour, plus extra for dusting
200 ml/7 fl oz lukewarm water
600 g/1 lb 5 oz fresh plum tomatoes
approx. 900 g/2 lb cime di rapa
6 tbsp extra virgin olive oil, plus extra for drizzling
4 garlic cloves, finely chopped
1 vegetable stockpot or cube
sea salt

First make the pasta. Place the flour in a large bowl or on a clean work surface, make a well in the centre and gradually add 200 ml/7 fl oz lukewarm water, mixing to make a soft dough. Knead lightly for a couple of minutes until smooth, then form into a ball and leave to rest while you prepare the other ingredients.

Using a sharp knife, make an incision at the top of each tomato, then place in a pan of boiling water for about a minute – this helps loosen the skin from the flesh. Drain, allow to cool a little, then remove the skin, cut in half and, with the help of a teaspoon, remove as many of the seeds as you can. Roughly chop the tomato flesh, keeping the juices.

Take the *cime di rapa* and remove and discard the stems. Bring a large pan of water to the boil, add the leaves and cook for about 5 minutes until tender, then drain (reserving the cooking water) and roughly chop.

Place the olive oil in a pan over a medium heat, sweat the garlic for about a minute, then stir in the tomato flesh with a little salt. Reduce the heat a little and cook, partially covered with a lid, for about 15 minutes until the juices reduce and you obtain a thick consistency. Increase the heat a little, stir in the cooked *cime di rapa* leaves with a little of the reserved cooking water and cook for 5 minutes, then remove from the heat and set aside.

To make the *surgi* shapes, take small pieces of the dough and roll into very long snake-like shapes, with a diameter of 5 mm (¼ inch) – for ease of rolling, moisten your hands with a little water. Cut lengths (approx. 6 cm/2½ inches), then, with your three middle fingers, press down firmly and roll over. Continue doing this until you have used up all the dough. As you work, place the *surgi* on a lightly floured board covered with a cloth to avoid the pasta drying out while you make the rest.

Bring the pan of *cime di rapa* cooking water back to the boil, then drop in the *surgi* and cook for about 10 minutes. In the meantime, place the pan with the tomatoes and greens back on the heat. Using a spider utensil or slotted spoon, transfer the *surgi* to the tomato sauce, along with about 8 ladles of cooking water, add the stockpot or crumble in the stock cube and cook over a medium–high heat for a further 10 minutes, until the pasta is cooked through.

Remove from the heat and serve immediately, drizzled with a little olive oil.

Cooking Tip
Cime di rapa is a leafy 'winter green' that tastes both sweet and slightly bitter. Often known as 'rape tops' in the UK, they can be found in international greengrocers and some markets. But if you can't find them, use spinach, kale or spring greens instead.

FRITTELLE UBALDINE

Medieval pancakes

The idea for this recipe comes from *Libro de la Cocina,* a 14th century cookbook by an anonymous Tuscan author, and a time when herbs and flowers were common ingredients in the kitchen. The original recipe uses a herb called nepitella, a type of mint, but as this is difficult to source, I have replaced it with a mix of regular mint, parsley and basil. You can use whichever brightly coloured edible flowers you can find at your greengrocer or specialist shop, like borage and nasturtiums. The original recipe also adds finely chopped onion but I have omitted this as you can then enjoy the *frittelle* as a sweet dish, adding just a pinch of salt and serving them with a drizzle of honey and a squeeze of lemon juice.

MAKES 5 PANCAKES

4 egg whites
150g/5½ oz self-raising flour, sifted
pinch of sea salt
½ handful of flat-leaf parsley, finely chopped
½ handful of mint, finely chopped
½ handful of basil, finely chopped
handful of edible flowers
knob of butter

In a large bowl, whisk the egg whites with a hand whisk, then gradually whisk in the flour, making sure there are no lumps. Add the pinch of salt and gently fold in the herbs and flowers.

Grease a small, non-stick frying pan with a knob of butter and place over a medium heat. When melted and hot, place a couple of dollops of the mixture into the pan and flatten slightly to make a pancake of approx. 10 cm/4 inches in diameter and 1 cm/½ inch thick, and cook for about 3 minutes on each side until golden. Remove and keep warm while you repeat with the remaining mixture. Serve immediately.

TORTA DI FARRO SALATA

Savoury spelt bake

This savoury spelt bake comes from the Garfagnana area of Tuscany, where this ancient grain has thrived for centuries and is used in all sorts of local dishes. Spelt is high in protein and fibre and, combined with eggs, cheese and fresh herbs, this simple dish makes a quick, nutritious meal at any time.

SERVES 4

- 100 g/3½ oz spelt
- 250 g/9 oz ricotta, well-drained
- 100 g/3½ oz grated Parmesan cheese
- 2 eggs, lightly beaten
- 1 tbsp mixed herbs, finely chopped (rosemary needles, thyme leaves, sage and flat-leaf parsley)
- extra virgin olive oil, for greasing
- rocket leaves, to serve
- sea salt and freshly ground black pepper

Preheat the oven to 160°C Fan/180°C/350°F/gas mark 4.

Bring a pan of water to the boil and cook the spelt until tender (check the instructions on the packet for precise cooking times), then drain.

Place the spelt in a bowl, mix with the ricotta, Parmesan, eggs and herbs, then season with salt and pepper to taste.

Grease a 20 cm/8 inch round cake tin or ovenproof dish with a little oil, then pour in the mixture and bake for 40 minutes until nicely browned and set. Serve immediately with a rocket salad.

CICORIA CACIO E OVA

Cicoria soup with cheese and eggs

This traditional rural soup is Abruzzo's version of the Roman *Stracciatella*, which adds eggs and cheese to leftover meat broth. To make the broth, I've used stock pots for speed and simplicity, but you could start from scratch and boil a chicken for an even more nutritious and satisfying winter warmer.

SERVES 4

400 g/14 oz wild chicory (or cavolo nero or spinach)
approx. 1.5 litres/2¾ pints chicken stock
1 small onion, finely chopped
1 celery stalk, roughly chopped
1 small carrot, roughly chopped
2 tbsp extra virgin olive oil
50 g/1¾ oz pancetta, finely chopped
1 small onion, finely chopped
6 eggs
120 g/4¼ oz grated Pecorino cheese
rustic bread, to serve
sea salt and freshly ground black pepper

Cut away any thick woody stalks from the chicory, if using, and rinse well in cold water. Bring a pot of water to the boil and blanch the chicory for a couple of minutes, then drain and soak in cold water for about 20 minutes, to remove as much of the bitterness as possible. After soaking, drain well, squeeze out any excess water with your hands, then place on a board, roughly chop and set aside.

In a large pot, place the chicken stock, onion, celery and carrot and bring to the boil, then lower the heat and cook for about 10 minutes, until the vegetables are cooked through.

Meanwhile, place the olive oil in a pan over a medium heat and sweat the pancetta and onion for about 5 minutes until softened. Stir in the chicory (or other leaves, if using), season with salt and pepper to taste, then continue to cook for a further 5 minutes.

In a small bowl, whisk together the eggs and grated Pecorino to a creamy consistency. Divide this mixture between 4 soup bowls, followed by the chicory (or other veg), pancetta and onion, and then ladle over the hot stock mixture.

Serve immediately with some rustic bread.

Ingredient Note
Cicoria or chicory is a popular green leafy vegetable and is often collected wild in central Italy. However, the cultivated variety is widely available in greengrocers and supermarkets. Its bitter taste and slightly serrated leaves resemble dandelion, which can also be used in this recipe. Otherwise, cavolo nero or spinach are good and quick substitutes, which won't need any additional soaking.

CHICHI'

Tuna and pickle pie

This curious filled focaccia from Offida in Le Marche is so popular in its hometown that it has its own *sagra* (food festival) dedicated to it every summer. The word *chichi'* in local dialect means 'filled pizza', but it can also mean 'piece of dough'. In the past, when making bread, mothers would give a piece of dough to the children to play with, and many say this is how the recipe was born. However, another theory claims it was made early in the morning to the *chichi'* sound of the cockerel. Whichever theory is true, if any, this ancient bake can be eaten hot or cold. Served with a green salad, it makes a lovely light meal.

SERVES 4–6

For the dough

14 g/½ oz fresh yeast
4½ tbsp lukewarm water
100 ml/3½ fl oz semi-skimmed or whole milk
2 tbsp extra virgin olive oil, plus extra for brushing
400 g/14 oz 00 flour
¾ tsp sea salt

For the filling

1 x 200 g/7 oz tin of tuna in olive oil
300 g/10½ oz giardiniera (Italian mixed vegetable pickles,) roughly chop any big pieces
4 anchovy fillets, finely chopped
2 tsp capers
120 g/4¼ oz pitted olives, quartered
handful of flat-leaf parsley, finely chopped

First make the dough. In a jug, dissolve the yeast in the lukewarm water, then combine with the milk and olive oil.

Place the flour and salt in a large bowl or stand mixer and gradually add the liquid yeast mixture, mixing well to form a dough. Knead for 5 minutes, then cover with a cloth and leave in a warm place for at least 1½ hours, until doubled in size.

In the meantime, in a bowl, combine all the filling ingredients, including the tuna oil.

Preheat the oven to 200°C Fan/220°C/425°F/gas mark 7.

Divide the dough in half and roll out each piece, as thinly as you can, into a roughly rectangular shape. Line a flat baking tray (30 x 22 cm/12 x 8½ inches) with baking paper and arrange one piece of dough on top. Spread the filling mixture all over, leaving a border of 1 cm/½ inch all around. Brush the edge with a little water, cover with the other piece of dough and press down along the edges to secure well. Prick all over the top with a fork and brush with a little olive oil, then bake in the oven for 20 minutes until golden.

Remove from the oven, leave to rest for 5 minutes, then slice and serve.

Ingredient Note

This is the perfect recipe for using up storecupboard ingredients. If you can't get *giardiniera*, use a variety of preserved vegetables, like peppers, baby onions, cornichons, cauliflower, artichokes or whatever you have available.

LA TORTA SALATA DI GAETA

Octopus pie

This unusual pie comes from the coastal town of Gaeta in Lazio, where it was traditionally eaten by fishermen, who needed nutritious and substantial food that would satisfy their hunger for a few days whilse at sea. The pastry is made with bread dough, as is traditional with most savoury Italian pies, and the fillings would vary, depending on the fishermen's catch and what other ingredients were available at the time. However, this is my favourite combination: octopus, olives and capers sandwiched between homemade bread dough is divine!

SERVES 4

For the dough
- 6 g/⅛ oz fresh yeast
- 160 ml/5¼ fl oz lukewarm water
- 300 g/10½ oz strong white bread flour, plus extra for dusting
- pinch of sea salt
- 1¼ tbsp extra virgin olive oil, plus extra for greasing

For the filling
- 2 tbsp extra virgin olive oil
- 2 anchovy fillets
- 1 garlic clove, crushed and left whole
- 750 g/1 lb 10 oz prepared fresh whole octopus
- 3¼ tbsp white wine
- 200 g/7 oz cherry tomatoes, halved
- 40 g/1½ oz black Gaeta olives, pitted
- 25 g/1 oz capers
- 1 tbsp finely chopped flat-leaf parsley

Recipe continues overleaf

First make the pastry/bread dough. Dilute the yeast in a little of the lukewarm water. In a large bowl, combine the flour and salt, then add the yeast mixture and olive oil and gradually mix with the remaining/160 ml/5¼ fl oz lukewarm water to make a dough. Knead for 10 minutes, then roll into a ball, cover with clingfilm or a cloth, and set aside to rest for at least 1 hour, until doubled in size.

Now make the filling. Place the olive oil in a large, deep-sided pan over a medium heat, add the anchovies and sweat the garlic for a minute, then discard. Holding the octopus by its head, dip the tentacles into the hot oil until the tentacles curl up, then place the whole octopus in the pan and stir-fry for a couple of minutes. Add the white wine and allow to evaporate, then add the tomatoes, olives, capers and parsley, stir-frying for a couple of minutes. Lower the heat, cover the pan with a lid and cook for about 45 minutes. When the octopus is tender, transfer to a chopping board and cut into small chunks, then return to the tomato mixture.

Preheat the oven to 180°C Fan/200°C/400°F/gas mark 6. Grease a round, shallow, loose-bottomed pie dish or flan tin (22 cm/8½ inches) with some olive oil and dust with a little flour.

Divide the dough into two, making one piece a little bigger. Roll out the bigger piece on a lightly floured work surface, line the pie dish, then fill with the octopus mixture. Roll out the remaining dough and place it over the top of the pie dish, crimping the edges together to secure well. Brush the top of the pastry with a little olive oil and bake in the oven for 30 minutes, until golden.

Remove the pie from the oven and leave to rest for 5 minutes, then serve.

Ingredient Notes
You can either source fresh octopus from your fishmonger or cheat with a quality ready-cooked variety, which are sold in vacuum packs and can be found in most Italian food shops. In this case, use 300 g/10½ oz, add with the tomatoes and cook for just 15 minutes. If you can't find Gaeta olives, try Taggiasca or Kalamata or any other black olives.

SURICITTI MARCHIGIANI

Polenta dumplings with sausage and broccoli

This rustic dish from Le Marche is a great way of using up leftover cooked polenta, which is made into little gnocchi-like dumplings. Traditionally, they were served with whatever was available, such as pork fat, pork ribs, sausages or simply with a grating of local Pecorino cheese. This is my version, with sausage and broccoli for a complete and nutritious meal.

SERVES 4–6

300 g/10½ oz long-stem broccoli

3 tbsp extra virgin olive oil, plus extra for drizzling

2 garlic cloves, crushed and left whole

400 g/14 oz Italian pork sausages, skin removed and crumbled into small pieces

500 g/1 lb 2 oz cooked polenta

200 g/7 oz 00 or plain flour

grated Parmesan or Pecorino cheese, to serve

sea salt and freshly ground black pepper

Bring a pan of water to the boil and parboil the broccoli for 4 minutes, then remove and drain well.

Place the olive oil in a pan over a medium heat and sweat the garlic cloves for a minute or so to infuse the oil, then discard. Add the crumbled sausagemeat and stir-fry for about 4 minutes, until coloured. Stir in the broccoli, cover with a lid and cook over a medium-low heat for about 10 minutes.

Meanwhile, place the cold polenta onto a clean work surface and, gradually incorporating the flour, knead into a smooth dough. Take pieces of the dough, roll into a sausage shape and cut out small dumplings, about 2.5 cm/1 inch in length.

Bring a large pot of salted water to the boil, drop in the dumplings and cook for 2–3 minutes until they float to the top. Pick them up with a spider utensil or slotted spoon and transfer to a serving dish or divide between individual bowls. Top with the sausage and broccoli mixture, sprinkle with grated cheese and a little black pepper, drizzle with olive oil and serve.

Cooking Tip

If you don't have leftover cooked polenta to hand, you can make it easily: Place 160 g/5¾ oz quick-cook polenta in a pan with approx. 650 ml/22 fl oz boiling water and cook, whisking. Check the instructions on the packet for precise cooking times. Leave to cool, then use as above.

ARROSTO DI STINCO CON SALSINA APICIUS

Roast pork shank with Apicius sauce

I discovered this example of Ancient Roman cuisine through the Historical Italian Cooking Blog, which quoted it from the Apicius, a collection of Roman recipes, which may date back to the 5th century. The original recipe uses a whole suckling pig and the herbs lovage and rue in the sauce. However, I have adapted this, preferring fennel seeds and rocket in place of rue, a very bitter herb no longer recommended as edible. In Ancient Rome, *garum* (a fermented fish sauce) was widely used as a condiment for this feast. The modern-day equivalent, *colatura di alici*, is made from fresh anchovies. It has quite a pungent flavour so should be used sparingly, but combined with runny honey, herbs and spices, it really works.

SERVES 2–3

abundant large bay leaves
1.3 kg/3 lb pork shank
extra virgin olive oil
roast potatoes, to serve
sea salt and freshly ground black pepper

For the sauce

1 tbsp fennel seeds
1 tbsp ground coriander
½ tsp freshly ground black pepper
30 g/1 oz rocket, finely chopped
½ handful of mint leaves, finely chopped
1 tbsp runny honey
1 tbsp white wine
2 tsp colatura di alici

Preheat the oven to 200°C Fan/220°C/425°F/gas mark 7 and line a roasting tin with bay leaves.

Rub the pork all over with olive oil, salt and pepper, then arrange in the roasting tin over the bay and roast for about 2½ hours, until cooked through.

In the meantime, prepare the sauce in a bowl. Grind the fennel seeds until you obtain a fine powder, then combine with the coriander and pepper. Add the rocket and mint, stir through the honey, wine and *Colatura di Alici*, then set aside. You could also do this in a small blender to make a really smooth sauce.

Remove the pork from the oven and leave to rest for about 5 minutes. To serve, carve into thin slices and pour over the sauce. Serve with roast potatoes.

Ingredient Note
If you like crackling, leave the skin on the pork shank, otherwise remove it with a sharp knife (you can ask your butcher to do this for you) before cooking.

Cooking Tip
The sauce tastes even better if made in advance so the flavours infuse nicely, preferably overnight. It's best kept in the fridge then served at room temperature when requried.

BUGLIONE TOSCANA DI TRE CARNI

Three-meat stew

In Tuscan dialect, the word *buglione* means 'a jumble', which is precisely what this stew has always signified. Originally a *cucina povera* dish, it threw everything into the pot, using whatever meat or vegetables were available, to feed a large family. Marinating helped soften cheaper cuts of meat and the addition of vinegar was commonly used to 'disinfect' any meat that might be going off. Nowadays, lamb is commonly used, but I've combined this with pork and beef to stay true to the 'jumble' ethos.

SERVES 4–6

400 g/14 oz stewing lamb
400 g/14 oz stewing pork
400 g/14 oz stewing beef
6 cloves
2 bay leaves
8 large sage leaves, 4 left whole, 4 finely chopped
1 large onion, finely chopped
2 celery stalks, finely chopped
2 carrots, finely chopped
150 ml/5fl oz red wine
1 tbsp red wine vinegar
5 tbsp extra virgin olive oil
2 garlic cloves, crushed and left whole
½ red chilli, finely sliced
2 rosemary sprigs
100 ml/3½ fl oz red wine
2 tbsp tomato purée
600 ml/1 pint hot vegetable stock
rustic bread, sliced and toasted, to serve
sea salt and freshly ground black pepper

In a large bowl, combine the lamb, pork and beef with the cloves, bay leaves, whole sage leaves, onion, celery, carrots, red wine and vinegar, then cover and leave to marinate in the fridge overnight.

When you are ready to cook, drain the meat and vegetables, discarding the liquid plus herbs and spices, and set aside.

In a large pan, warm 3 tablespoons of olive oil over a low heat and sweat the garlic cloves for a minute to infuse the oil, then discard them. Increase the heat to medium, add the meat, chilli, rosemary and the chopped sage and seal the meat well all over. Add the red wine and allow to evaporate.

Transfer the meat to a plate and set aside. Place the remaining olive oil in the pan over a medium heat and sweat the reserved onion, celery and carrots (from the marinade) for a few minutes until softened. Return the meat to the pan, heat through, then season with a little salt and pepper.

Dissolve the tomato purée into the hot vegetable stock, then pour this over the meat in the pan. Bring to the boil, then reduce the heat, cover with a lid and gently cook for 1½ hours.

After this time, remove the lid and continue to cook for about 15 minutes to reduce and thicken the sauce a little.

Serve immediately with lightly toasted slices of rustic bread.

Cooking Tip:
This dish does require a little forward-planning as the meat needs to marinate in the fridge overnight.

CROSTATA DI RICOTTA E VISCIOLE

Ricotta and cherry tart

This delicious tart comes from Roman Jewish cuisine and was originally made without a pastry top. However, in the 1700s, harsh papal rules prohibited the sale of dairy products by Jews to Christians, and so ingenious Jewish bakers came up with the idea of covering the ricotta with a pastry top, so as not to arouse suspicion. This cheesecake is still made in the Jewish Quarter in Rome today, in an old traditional bakery.

SERVES 6

220 g/8 oz 00 flour, plus extra for dusting

100 g/3½ oz butter, cut into small pieces, plus extra for greasing

70 g/2½ oz caster sugar

pinch of ground cinnamon

zest of ½ lemon

1 tsp vanilla extract

2 egg yolks, lightly beaten

For the filling

500 g/1 lb 2 oz ricotta, well-drained

80 g/2¾ oz caster sugar

180 g/6¼ oz cherry jam

1 egg yolk, beaten with a little milk, for egg wash

icing sugar, for dusting

In a large bowl, place the flour and butter and rub together with your fingertips until the mixture resembles breadcrumbs. Stir in the sugar, cinnamon, lemon zest and vanilla extract, then gradually fold in the egg yolks, until the mixture comes together to form a soft pastry dough. If necessary, add a little cold water. Form into a ball, wrap in clingfilm and place in the fridge to rest for 30 minutes.

In the meantime, preheat the oven to 160°C Fan/180°C/350°F/gas mark 4. Butter a round pie dish/tin (22 cm/8½ inches in diameter) and lightly dust with flour.

In a bowl, mix the ricotta and sugar for the filling until nice and creamy, then cover and store in the fridge.

Divide the dough into two pieces, one slightly bigger than the other and, on a lightly floured surface, roll out each piece into a circle, approx. 5 mm/¼ inch thick. Line the prepared pie dish/tin with the larger piece, spread this with the jam and top with the ricotta mixture. Cover with the other pastry circle, brush the edges with a little water, crimping to secure well, so the filling doesn't escape. Brush the top with egg wash and bake in the oven for about 50 minutes, until golden.

Remove from the oven and allow to cool in the dish/tin.

Carefully remove the pie from the dish/tin, sprinkle with sifted icing sugar and serve.

Ingredient Note
The original recipe uses sour cherries, hence the *visciole* in the Italian title, but I have used a regular cherry jam, which is easily obtainable.

PAN DUCALE

Almond and chocolate loaf cake

As the name suggests, *Pan Ducale* ('bread of the duke'), from the Abruzzo region, has ancient and noble origins. It was first made for the Duke of Acquaviva in the town of Atri in 1352 to celebrate *Festum Pacis*, the 'feast of peace', and the duke ordered it to be sent to all the neighbouring dukes in the region as a sign of friendship. Today, the cake is still a taste of Abruzzo and is sold in shops throughout the region. This is my homemade version, which is deceptively light but also rich and nutritious; perfect to enjoy with an espresso or cup of tea.

MAKES 1 LOAF CAKE – SERVES 8–10

2 eggs, separated
130 g/4¾ oz golden caster sugar or light brown soft sugar
1 tsp vanilla extract
zest of 1 orange
40 g/1½ oz candied fruit peel, finely chopped
90 g/3¼ oz blanched almonds, lightly toasted and finely chopped
100 g/3½ oz dark chocolate, finely chopped or grated
pinch of sea salt
½ tsp ground cinnamon
70 g/2½ oz butter, melted
120 g/4¼ oz 00 flour, sifted
1 x 16 g /1½ oz sachet of Paneangeli – or 3½ tsp baking powder

Preheat the oven to 160°C Fan/180°C/350°F/gas mark 4 and line a 900 g/2 lb loaf tin with baking paper.

In a bowl, whisk together the egg yolks and sugar until light and pale in colour. Stir in the vanilla extract, orange zest, candied peel, almonds, chocolate, salt, cinnamon and melted butter, then fold in the flour and Paneangeli. The mixture will be quite dense but that's ok.

In a separate bowl, whisk the egg whites until stiff, then fold these into the cake mixture.

Spoon the mixture into the prepared loaf tin and bake in the oven for 50–55 minutes. Check that the cake is cooked by inserting a skewer into the middle – if it comes out dry, then it's ready.

Allow the cake to cool slightly, then tip it out of the tin onto a serving plate or board and serve immediately.

BISCOTTI BIRBI

Almond biscuits

The recipe for these age-old biscuits comes from the nuns of the Sant'Agnese convent in Rieti, in the Lazio region. These days, just a handful of nuns live at the convent and, according to Anna Maria Foli's *La Cucina Come Una Volta*, they dedicate their time to prayer, their allotment and to the production of communion hosts for nearby churches, so these biscuits are probably no longer made. Light, crunchy and extremely simple to make, they are perfect for anyone on a gluten-free diet.

MAKES 20

2 egg whites
pinch of sea salt
70 g/2½ oz caster sugar
pinch of ground cinnamon
80 g/2¾ oz blanched almonds, roughly chopped
20 g/¾ oz pine kernels
zest of ½ lemon

Preheat the oven to 140°C Fan/160°C/325°F/gas mark 3, and line a large, flat baking tray with baking paper.

In a bowl, whisk the egg whites with the salt until stiff. Fold in the sugar, cinnamon, almonds, pine kernels and lemon zest.

Place small dollops of the mixture onto the lined baking tray, spacing them about 2 cm/¾ inch apart, then bake for 30 minutes until very lightly golden.

Serve immediately or, if stored in an airtight container, they will keep for at least a week.

SFRATTO DI GOYM

Honey and walnut pastry roll

This age-old Jewish recipe is linked to the hilltop town of Pitigliano where, in the 1620s, the Grand Duke Cosimo II de' Medici forced Jews from all over Tuscany into a ghetto. Tuscan landlords evicted Jewish tenants and would arrive at their homes with sticks to bang on doors. About a century later, the Jewish bakers of Pitigliano came up with the idea of this filled sweet treat, made in the shape of a stick, and named it *Sfratto di Goym*, which translates as 'eviction of the goyim (non-Jewish person)'. Although only a handful of the population of Pitigliano is now Jewish, this traditional, symbolic pastry can still be found at the local bakery and is a product recognized by the Slow Food Association.

SERVES 6

For the pastry
- 200 g/7 oz 00 flour, plus extra for dusting
- pinch of sea salt
- 100 g/3½ oz hard butter, cut into small pieces
- 75 g/2¾ oz caster sugar
- 2 egg yolks, lightly beaten, plus 1 egg yolk, beaten with a little milk, for egg wash

For the filling
- 175 ml/6 fl oz runny honey
- 175 g/6 oz walnuts, finely chopped
- zest of 1 orange
- pinch of ground nutmeg

Preheat the oven to 180°C Fan/200°C/400°F/gas mark 6, and line a baking tray with baking paper.

First make the pastry. In a large bowl, place the flour, salt and butter and rub together with your fingertips until the mixture resembles breadcrumbs. Stir in the sugar. Gradually add the beaten egg yolks and mix well to obtain a soft, smooth pastry dough – if necessary, add a drop of cold water. Form into a ball, wrap in clingfilm or a cloth and leave to rest in the fridge while you make the filling.

In a small pan, gently heat the honey, walnuts, orange zest and nutmeg for about 4 minutes, stirring all the time, until the mixture has slightly thickened and the ingredients are combined. Remove from the heat and set aside to cool.

On a lightly floured surface, roll out the pastry into a rectangle shape (approx. 30 x 20 cm/12 x 8 inches). Spread the filling over the pastry, leaving a little border around the edge, then roll up to make a long log, securing the ends so the filling doesn't escape.

Transfer the pastry roll to the lined baking tray, brush with egg wash and bake in the oven for 25 minutes, until golden.

Remove from the oven, leave to cool slightly on the baking tray, then slice and serve.

Ingredient Note
The original pastry is made with white wine and olive oil instead of butter. However, I like to use butter for a slightly softer sweet shortcrust pastry.

CUSCNIEDD (CALZONCELLI DI CECI E CIOCCOLATO)

Chickpea and chocolate pastries

These unusual ravioli-type sweet pastries come from Lucania, in the mountainous region of Basilicata. It was a tradition, in the old days, to make something sweet for Christmas out of whatever ingredients were to hand during the lean winter months, hence the main ingredient of chickpeas, which was a common rural legume. The recipe has evolved over time with additional ingredients, like cocoa powder to provide a chocolate taste, and the fillings can vary, but this is my favourite version of the little pastries, which are known as *cuscniedd* in local dialect, meaning little cushions.

MAKES APPROX. 28 PASTRIES

For the pastry
250 g/9 oz 00 flour, plus extra for dusting
25 g/1 oz caster sugar
3¼ tbsp extra virgin olive oil
1 egg, lightly beaten
2 tbsp white wine

For the filling
1 x 400 g/14 oz tin of chickpeas, drained and rinsed
1⅓ tbsp espresso coffee powder
zest of 1 clementine
1 tbsp runny honey
2 tbsp dark rum
20 g/¾ oz cocoa powder
10 g/¼ oz pine kernels

abundant vegetable or sunflower oil, for frying
icing sugar, for dusting

First make the pastry. In a large bowl, combine the flour and sugar, then stir in the olive oil, beaten egg and white wine and work into a smooth pastry dough. Roll into a ball, wrap in clingfilm or a cloth and leave to rest in the fridge for an hour.

Meanwhile, prepare the filling. In a blender, blend together the chickpeas, espresso coffee powder, clementine zest, honey, rum and cocoa powder until smooth. Stir through the pine kernels, then set aside.

Take the pastry out of the fridge and give it a quick knead to return it to room temperature. On a lightly floured surface, roll out the pastry to about 5 mm/¼ inch thick – or use the no. 2 setting on a pasta machine.

Using a 10-cm/4-inch cookie cutter, cut the dough into circles, then place a dollop of filling in the centre of each. Brush the edges with a little water, then fold over, pressing down well to make half-moon shapes. Use a fork to crimp and secure the edges or pinch them together with your thumb and index finger.

Heat abundant oil in a heavy-based pan and fry the *cuscniedd* in batches, a few at a time, for 2–3 minutes on each side until golden. Using a spider utensil or slotted spoon, transfer to kitchen paper, cool, then sprinkle with sifted icing sugar.

Serve immediately or, if stored in an airtight container, they will keep for at least a week.

BUDINO DI CASTAGNE

Chestnut puddings

This pudding is common in northern regions and especially Piemonte, which borders with France and so its foods often reflect the influence of French cuisine. Wobbly creamy puddings, like the French Crème Caramel and *Bavarois* have led to Piemontese versions like *Bonet*, *Bavarese* and the classic *Montebianco*, a purée of chestnuts with double cream on top to look like Mont Blanc. My version of a chestnut pudding is simple to make, like a thick custard that you leave to set in the fridge, and is delicious served with crunchy amaretti biscuits, pine kernels and chocolate shavings.

MAKES 4 INDIVIDUAL PUDDINGS

4 egg yolks
140 g/5 oz caster sugar
100 g/3½ oz chestnut flour, sifted
500 ml/18 fl oz semi-skimmed or whole milk
2 dsp dark rum

To decorate
approx. 6 small amaretti biscuits
handful of pine kernels
dark chocolate shavings

In a heatproof bowl, whisk together the egg yolks and sugar until light and paler in colour. Gradually whisk in the chestnut flour, until well incorporated. Heat the milk gently in a non-stick saucepan until warm, then gradually pour it into the chestnut mixture, whisking well to avoid any lumps.

Pour the mixture back into the same saucepan, place over a medium heat and cook for a few minutes, whisking all the time, until the mixture thickens and begins to bubble. Remove from the heat and stir in the rum.

Moisten the inside of 4 individual serving glasses (6 cm/2½ inches in diameter) and divide the mixture between them. Leave to cool, then place in the fridge for at least an hour to set.

Crumble the amaretti biscuits over the top, sprinkle with the pine kernels and some chocolate shavings and serve.

Ingredient Note
Chestnuts have always been popular all over Italy but especially in the *cucina povera* of rural areas. Easily foraged, they provided much-needed nutrition and were often ground into flour to make bread and pasta.

ISLANDS

When we think of Italian islands, Sicily and Sardinia immediately spring to mind, but there are many more, and each contributes unique flavours to the rich diversity of Italian food and culture.

Sicily, the largest of the Italian islands, is surrounded by the warm waters of the southern Mediterranean Sea and enjoys a very balmy climate all year round. This makes it excellent for growing wonderful produce like aubergines, peppers, Pachino tomatoes, olives, vines, almonds and citrus fruits – their blood-red oranges simply are the best! Some of the biggest and best tuna and swordfish are caught along the Sicilian coast, as well as an array of other Mediterranean fish.

Although extremely close to the mainland, Sicily has its own distinct feel and culture, reflecting its rich and eventful history as a strategic outpost in Mediterranean waters. As such, it was the perfect stopping place for all who sailed the sea and the Greeks, Romans, Arabs, Normans and Spanish have all left their mark on Sicilian culture, architecture and, of course, its food. In fact, Sicilian cuisine is probably the most eclectic of all Italian food. Many dishes use couscous and ingredients such as almonds, raisins, cinnamon and many other spices, which reveal the influence of North Africa. The Arabs are also said to have introduced ice cream to the island, as well as many sweet treats. These days, ice cream and granita are still the highlight of any visit to Sicily and the speciality *Brioche al Tuppo* or *Brioche col Tuppo* – a brioche filled with ice cream – is often served for an indulgent breakfast treat!

Nothing shouts Sicily more than the island's wonderful desserts, such as indulgent ricotta-filled *cannoli* and beautifully decorated *cassata* cakes. *Frutta Martorana* are also an unforgettable local speciality – marzipan that has been coloured with natural dyes and modelled to resemble fruit and vegetables, so life-like you can't help but think you are biting into a cob of corn or a slice of watermelon! And the wonderful citrus fruits of Sicily are also candied and added to many local pastries and cakes.

Street food is very popular in Sicily, especially in the bustling food markets of Palermo with their array of *arancini*, *panelle* (chickpea fritters), *Pane ca Meusa* (spleen sandwich!), sweet and sour *caponata*, *Sarde a Beccafico* (see page 94), swordfish *involtini* and so much more. A feast for the eyes and palate!

All around Sicily are smaller islands, clustered in little groups. The Aeolian archipelago is made up of seven small islands and these are home to some of the best capers, which enhance many of the local dishes like *Pane Cunziato*, a summery panino filled wih local cheese, tomatoes, olives and capers, all drizzled with extra virgin olive oil. Off the west coast of Sicily are the Egadi Islands and fresh fish and seafood rule. Fish soup served with couscous and *Polpette di Tonno* (tuna balls) are a speciality of Favignana. These *polpette* originated in the tuna factory in the early 1900s by the women who worked there. They would make the *polpette* using the lesser cuts of tuna, which would otherwise have been thrown out, adding stale bread, eggs, garlic and herbs. As with much traditonal *cucina povera* food, this is now a popular dish in the island's restaurants. On the island of Marettima, to the west of Sicily, a classic dish is pasta cooked in a lobster broth.

Further south, and closer to Africa than Europe, lies the black volcanic island of Pantelleria. This is probably where North African culture has had the greatest influence, from its *dammusi* houses to dishes like *Sciakisciuka* (Sicilian shakshuka) – also known as *Ciaki Ciuka* (which, translated from North African, means a mix or melange) – it's a mixed vegetable stew of courgettes, aubergines and peppers cooked with tomatoes and often boiled eggs are added for protein. With a North African influence, it's gently warmed by the addition of red pepper flakes. *Cubbaita* is a nougat-type of sweet treat with North African origin which now forms part of the culinary tradition of this island. Made with honey, almonds, orange peel and sesame seeds, it is often served at the end of a meal with a glass of sweet Pantelleria wine.

A jewel in the glistening Mediterranean Sea, the island of Pantelleria is covered in farmland and farmers make up its population, as opposed to fishermen. The land has been carefully developed to grow capers, citrus fruits and Zibibbo grapes for the production of sweet wine. Over time, the locals have ingeniously designed walled enclosures to nurture citrus trees. Known as *Giardino Pantesco*, these circular stone enclosures protect the trees from constant winds which would otherwise not allow the lemons or oranges to thrive.

Islands 67

The fourth group of islands, known as the Pelagie, are made up of Lampedusa, Linosa and the uninhabited Lampione. Here the crystalline water brings in an abundance of the freshest fish and seafood. Like Pantelleria, they lie closer to Tunisia than Italy, and North African dishes are evident in the cuisine, which is rich with fish and couscous dishes, as well as delicious desserts to end the meal, like *Basboussa*, a sponge cake made with durum wheat semolina and ground almonds, soaked in an orange flower water.

Of course, Sardinia is also surrounded by turquoise seas and yet, curiously, fish and seafood have not played a major role in Sardinian cuisine. Historically, the island was vulnerable to attack by outsiders and so Sardinians preferred to live inland, surrounded by rugged mountains for protection, and tending their sheep. Far-removed from mainland Italy, Sardinian farmers and shepherds depended on what the land could provide and their cuisine, in the *cucina povera* tradition, reflects this. However, the longevity of the island's population is a testament to the quality of their produce and the status of Sardinia in one of the world's 'blue zones'.

The history of Sardinia can be traced back millions of years, with archaeological evidence suggesting prehistoric settlement. Due to its strategic central position in the western Mediterranean, the island, like Sicily, had several invaders over the centuries. In the 8th century BCE, Phoenicians founded cities, followed by the Carthaginians, Romans, Saracens, Spanish and the French under the House of Savoy, which ruled Piemonte in Northern Italy. Each left their mark and shaped rich traditions in the island's culture and food.

Sardinia is especially known for its beautifully intricate pasta shapes, such as *malloreddus* (see page 82), *lorighittas* (see page 78) and *culurzones* – a filled pasta with potato, local cheese and mint. *Filindeu* are very fine strands of pasta which are then laid across a wooden tray, followed by another layer placed over the top before a third layer is added. They are left to dry out, eventually resembling an exquisite piece of lace. Traditionally cooked in a mutton broth and served with fresh Pecorino cheese, it is a very ancient pasta dish made in the Nuoro region of the island and a real labour of love. Another ancient Sardininan pasta is *fregula*, or *fregola*. At first glance it looks like large pieces of couscous; made with durum wheat semolina, they are shaped into little balls and toasted, them giving it a beige to brown colour. Often cooked in a broth, *fregula* is served with vegetable and seafood sauces and cooked like a risotto.

Main dishes are often meat-based. Suckling pig, roasted on a spit, is a favourite for festive occasions and, for everyday meals, lamb or goat is popular, as well as dairy products like the mature hard cheeses Pecorino and Casu Marzu, as well as softer varieties for desserts like classic honey-drizzled *seadas*. The hillsides are full of herbs and bushes of *mirto* (myrtle) and this is not only used to flavour dishes, but is also made into a classic Sardinian liqueur of the same name – Mirto. Reddish purple in colour, it has a bitter taste and is served as a *digestivo* (digestive) at the end of a meal. Local breads are plentiful, such as bread rolls called *coccoi* (see page 104), which can be plain or filled, and the classic *Pane Carasau*, also known as *Carta da Musica*, which the shepherds used to take for a packed lunch in the mountains. This dry, wafer-thin flatbread can be made into lasagne-type dishes using the flatbread instead of pasta sheets (see page 108).

Although nowadays you are able to enjoy fresh fish in Sardinia, it is the dried variety that is the highly prized gourmet's treat. *Bottarga* (preserved tuna roe) is delicately shaved over pasta dishes and *mosciame di tonno* (air-dried tuna) is thinly sliced and served as a light starter in most high-end restaurants all over the island.

The third largest Italian island, Elba, lies just off the coast of Tuscany and is probably best known for Napolean's exile in the early 1800s. Its local cuisine is very influenced by Tuscan cooking, with thick bean soups, *cacciucco*, a fish stew popular along the Tuscan coast, and *stoccafisso* (dried fish). However, like the other islands, Elba's history and culture is influenced by a long series of invasions, and *Schiacca Briaca*, a Middle Eastern sweet cake made with dried fruit, nuts and local sweet wine is still eaten today, as is *gurguglione* – a ratatouille-type vegetable stew, and *imbollita* – age-old pastries made with figs.

Further south off the Naples coast, we come to the islands of Capri, Ischia and Procida. They are almost like a continuation of the Neapolitan and Amalfi coasts, with mountains and lush green coastal plains. The food on these islands is influenced by Campania and the fertile terraces and land are excellent for growing lemons, vines and lush tomatoes. Where Capri caters for sophisticated tourists with dishes of lobster and langoustine, Ischian food tends to be more rural with its famous *Coniglio all'Ischitana* – rabbit stew (see page 98).

On the other side, off the coast of Puglia, is the archipelago known as the Isole Tremiti. These jewels of the Adriatic are part of the Gargano National Park, with wild expanses of lush, dense pine forests and an undergrowth of hardy herbs like juniper, rosemary and myrtle. The islands are not inhabited all year round and tend to be used for summer holidays. Food here tends to revolve around fresh fish and the abundant seafood of the Adriatic Sea.

Heading north are the Venetian *isolotti*, which include Burano, Murano, Torcello and Giudecca – all who rely on the fish of the *laguna* to eat and sell and which greatly influences the cuisine of the Venice area, like the popular *Risotto al Nero di Sepia* (squid ink risotto), seafood soups, grilled eel, prawns, giant plates of *fritto misto* among many others.

In spite of all the differences and various specialities of the islands from north to south, one thing which unites them all is that the produce has not travelled far and whatever you are eating will be local, the freshest and the best.

PASTA ALL'ANCIOVA E MUDDICA

Pasta with anchovies and breadcrumbs

This traditional dish from Palermo is linked to the migration of many Sicilians to Northern Italy in search of work, and so is often called *La Pasta Milanisa* (the Milanese pasta). They brought with them long-lasting ingredients from home, like preserved salted anchovies, homemade tomato *estratto* (a rich concentrate) and dried fruit, and would make dishes like this one to remind them of the sunshine of the South, while living in the cool and often foggy darkness of Milan in the winter.

SERVES 4

16 anchovy fillets in salt (approx. 60 g/2¼ oz in total)
3 tbsp extra virgin olive oil
2 garlic cloves, finely chopped
2 small shallots, finely chopped
120 g/4¼ oz tomato purée
300 g/10½ oz bucatini
sea salt
20 g/¾ oz sultanas, soaked in a little lukewarm water then drained
10 g/¼ oz pine kernels
handful of flat-leaf parsley, finely chopped
20 g/¾ oz dried breadcrumbs

Rinse the anchovy fillets in water to remove the salt, then pat dry and set aside.

In a pan, heat 2 tablespoons olive oil over a medium heat and sweat the garlic and shallots for a couple of minutes until softened. Add the anchovy fillets and continue to cook for a couple of minutes until they have dissolved. Add the tomato purée and cook over a low heat for about 10 minutes, until it begins to thicken slightly.

In the meantime, cook the bucatini in a separate pan of boiling salted water until 'al dente'.

In a smaller frying pan, heat the remaining olive oil over a medium heat and, when hot, lightly toast the breadcrumbs, stirring for about a minute. Remove from the heat and set aside.

Drain the pasta and add to the anchovy and tomato sauce along with a little of the hot pasta water. Cook over a medium heat, mixing well, for a minute or so.

Remove from the heat, sprinkle with the sultanas, pine kernels, parsley and toasted breadcrumbs and serve immediately.

Ingredient Notes
Salted anchovy fillets can be found in good Italian delis or online. Please use the best tomato purée you can (not tinned or passata) as this, together with the anchovies, will impart a depth of flavour and richness to the dish, which is balanced by the sweetness of the shallots and sultanas. The addition of pine kernels and lightly toasted breadcrumbs adds a nice crunchiness.

BUSIATE CON PESTO TRAPANESE

Busiate pasta with Trapani pesto

Busiate is a curly ringlet pasta shape from the western coastal town of Trapani in Sicily. It was originally made using a plant stem, known as *buso* in local dialect, hence the name *busiate*. They can be served with simple tomato sauces and ragùs, but I like to use the local pesto of the region, *Trapanese*, which has ancient origins. The story goes that Genovese basil pesto was introduced to Sicily by Ligurian sailors stopping at Trapani port and this inspired the locals to make their own version using local almonds and tomatoes, which results in a beautiful yellow-orange colour and a nice nutty crunch.

SERVES 4

400 g/14 oz durum wheat semolina flour (semola rimacinata), plus extra for dusting

200 ml/7 fl oz lukewarm water

For the pesto

75 g/2¾ oz blanched almonds

400 g/14 oz fresh plum tomatoes

bunch of basil leaves (approx. 50 g/1¾ oz)

2 small garlic cloves, peeled

20 g/¾ oz grated Pecorino cheese, plus extra for sprinkling

3 tbsp extra virgin olive oil

sea salt and freshly ground black pepper

First make the pasta dough. Place the flour in a large bowl or on a clean work surface, make a well in the centre and gradually add 200 ml/7 fl oz lukewarm water, mixing to make a soft dough. Knead lightly until smooth, then form into a ball and leave to rest at room temperature, covered with a cloth, for about 45 minutes.

In the meantime, prepare the pesto. In a small, dry frying pan, lightly toast the almonds over a medium heat, then remove and set aside. Using a sharp knife, make an incision at the top of each tomato, then place in a pan of boiling water for about a minute – this helps loosen the skin. Drain, allow to cool, then remove the skin, cut in half and, using a teaspoon, remove as many of the seeds as you can.

In a blender, place the almonds, tomatoes, basil leaves and garlic and whiz until you obtain a fairly smooth consistency. Add the grated Pecorino and olive oil, season to taste, then whiz quickly again until well combined. Set aside.

Divide the dough into six pieces and cover with a cloth so they don't dry out while you work. Take one piece of dough and, on a lightly floured surface, roll out with your hands into a long snake-like shape, as thin as you can. Cut out lengths of 10 cm/4 inches, then wrap each around a thin skewer to make a curly shape, resembling ringlets. Carefully transfer the *busiate* to a lightly floured board and cover again while you make the rest.

Bring a large pot of salted water to the boil and cook the *busiate* for 20–25 minutes, until cooked through. Drain the pasta, transfer to a bowl and toss with the pesto until thoroughly coated. Serve immediately with a sprinkling of extra Pecorino.

LORIGHITTAS CON FRUTTI DI MARE

Lorighittas pasta with seafood

Lorighittas is a handmade pasta from the village of Morgongiori in western Sardinia and this recipe has been passed down through multiple generations of women, who would traditionally get together and make the pasta for the feast of All Saints on 1st November. The literal translation is 'iron rings', and some believe these refer to the rings that were commonly attached to the walls of local houses to tie up horses, while others say they resemble the braided hoop earrings worn by the women. Like most dough and pastry work in Sardinia, *Lorighittas* is very intricate – they do take a little time to make, but the process is therapeutic; it's something you could do on a rainy day with family and friends.

SERVES 4

¾ tsp sea salt	splash of white wine
150 ml/5 fl oz lukewarm water	2 garlic cloves, left whole and squashed
300 g/10½ oz durum wheat semolina flour (semola rimacinata), plus extra for dusting	2 tbsp extra virgin olive oil
	½ red chilli, finely chopped (optional)
	200 g/7 oz calamari, sliced, keep tentacles intact
For the sauce	200 g/7 oz king prawns, shell on
500 g/1 lb 2 oz fresh mussels, washed, debearded and any open shells discarded	handful of flat-leaf parsley, finely chopped
	knob of butter
500 g/1 lb 2 oz fresh clams, washed and any open shells discarded	sea salt

Recipe continues overleaf

First make the pasta. Dilute the salt in 150 ml/5 fl oz lukewarm water. Place the flour in a large bowl or on a clean work surface, make a well in the centre and gradually add the salty water, mixing to make a soft dough. Knead lightly for a couple of minutes until smooth. Wrap in clingfilm or cover with a cloth and set aside to rest for 30 minutes.

Take small pieces of the dough (approx. 60g/2¼ oz) and roll into very long snake-like shapes, as thin as you can. Cut 20–22 cm/8–8½ inch lengths and wrap each around your middle 3 middle fingers twice, then pinch the ends to secure and twist the two layers of dough around each other to make a braided ring. As each one is made, place on a lightly floured board and cover with a cloth or clingfilm to avoid them drying out.

In a large saucepan, place the cleaned mussels and clams with a splash of white wine and one garlic clove. Cover with a tight-fitting lid and cook over a medium heat for about 4 minutes until the mussel and clam shells have opened. Discard any that have not opened. Remove from the heat and, when cool enough to handle, remove the flesh from most of the shells, keeping a few for garnishing. Pass the cooking liquid through a fine sieve and set aside.

In a large frying pan, heat the olive oil over a medium heat and sauté the remaining garlic clove and chilli, if using, for a few seconds, then increase the heat a little and stir-fry the calamari for about 10 minutes until tender. Add the prawns and continue to cook for about 4 minutes until cooked. Stir through the mussels, clams and half the parsley.

In the meantime, bring a large pot of salted water to the boil, drop in the *lorighittas* and cook for 4 minutes. With the help of a spider utensil or slotted spoon, transfer the pasta to the pan of seafood, along with a little of the strained liquid. Finish cooking the *lorighittas* this way, adding more liquid when necessary for about 2 or 3 minutes.

When the pasta is cooked, add a knob of butter and cook over a medium-high heat for about a minute or so, shaking the pan until you obtain a nice creamy consistency. Remove from the heat, add the remaining parsley and serve immediately.

MALLOREDDUS ALLA CAMPIDANESE

Sardinian malloreddus pasta with sausage and creamy Pecorino

Malloreddus has ancient origins in Sardinia and is still often made at home on Sundays and special occasions. It uses a typical Sardinian pasta, known as *gnocchetti sardi* in other parts of Italy for its gnocchi-like shape. If you don't have time to make your own, this pasta can be found dried in Italian delis or online.

SERVES 4

For the dough

400 g/14 oz durum wheat semolina flour (semola rimacinata), plus extra for dusting

200 ml/7 fl oz cold tap water

For the sauce

3 tbsp extra virgin olive oil

1 large onion, finely chopped

2 bay leaves

400 g/14 oz Italian pork sausages, skin removed

50 ml/3¼ tbsp white wine

400 ml/14 fl oz tomato passata

200 g/7 oz soft Pecorino cheese, grated

sea salt and freshly ground black pepper

Make the dough. In a large bowl, place the flour and gradually add the water, mixing to make a soft dough. Form into a ball, cover with clingfilm and leave to rest for 30 minutes.

Meanwhile, make the sauce. In a pan, heat the olive oil over a medium heat and sweat the onion with the bay leaves for a couple of minutes. Crumble in the sausage meat and stir-fry until the onion has softened and the sausage meat is coloured.

Add the white wine and allow to evaporate. Add the tomato passata along with a little water from rinsing out the jar or carton. Season with salt before covering with a lid and gently cooking for 25 minutes. Keep the sauce hot while you shape and cook the pasta.

Take about a quarter of the dough (leaving the rest covered to avoid it drying out) and, on a lightly floured surface, roll into very long snake-like shapes, as thin as you can. Cut out 1 cm /½ inch pieces, then place these onto a butter pat and, pressing down with your finger, roll downwards so they resemble gnocchi. Repeat until you have used all of the pasta dough.

Bring a large pot of salted water to the boil, drop in the *malloreddus* and cook for about 4 minutes.

Place the grated Pecorino in a small bowl and blend with about 6 tablespoons of the hot pasta water to obtain a creamy consistency.

Using a spider utensil or slotted spoon, transfer the *malloreddus* to the sausage sauce and stir to incorporate. Add the creamy Pecorino and cook over a medium-high heat for about a minute until the pasta and sauce are well combined. Remove from the heat and serve immediately.

CASCA' DI CARLOFORTE

Sardinian couscous with vegetables

This Tunisian-inspired couscous comes from the tiny Sardinian island of Carloforte. In the Middle Ages, this island was populated by the Ligurian people, who colonized the town of Tabarka in Tunisia and introduced new ingredients into Italian cuisine. Healthy and packed with vitamins, this dish is full of the flavours of North Africa and, with quick-cook couscous, makes a delicious meal at any time.

SERVES 4

- 3 tbsp vegetable or sunflower oil, for frying
- 1 large aubergine, cut into small cubes
- 2 tbsp extra virgin olive oil, plus extra for drizzling
- 1 onion, finely sliced
- 350 g/12 oz cauliflower florets
- ½ tsp fennel seeds
- 2 tbsp hot water
- 1 large carrot, sliced and parboiled
- 130 g/4¾ oz frozen broad beans
- 1 x 400 g/14 oz tin of chickpeas, drained and rinsed
- 2 tbsp mixed ground spices, e.g. turmeric, coriander, cumin, paprika
- 250 g/9 oz quick-cook couscous
- zest of 1 lemon

In a deep and heavy-based pan, heat the frying oil over a medium-high heat until hot, then shallow-fry the aubergine for about 5 minutes until cooked and golden all over. Transfer to kitchen paper to drain.

Heat the olive oil over a medium heat in a clean pan and sweat the onion until softened. Stir in the cauliflower florets with the fennel seeds, add a couple of tablespoons of hot water, cover the pan with a lid and cook for about 5 minutes. Add the parboiled carrots, broad beans and chickpeas and continue to cook for about 10 minutes until all the vegetables are cooked through but not mushy. Add the fried aubergine cubes to the pan and stir through with a tablespoon of the mixed spices. Keep warm.

Prepare the couscous according to the instructions on the packet, then fluff up with a fork and place on a serving dish. Top with the vegetables and sprinkle with the remaining mixed spices. Scatter the lemon zest over the top, drizzle with olive oil and serve.

Ingredient Note
In Sardinia, cooking is very seasonal, so use whatever vegetables are fresh and available.

BORDATINO

Polenta soup

This thick soup comes from Isola d'Elba, the small island off the coast of Tuscany, but there are also many variations from the mainland. According to tradition, the dish was originally made with buckwheat and seafood broth, as it was created by the sailors who transported the grain on their ships. Over time, the recipe evolved to use polenta flour, beans and cabbage, which provided sustenance for workers who travelled to the Tuscan island during the winter months to cultivate the land.

SERVES 2–4

150 g/5½ oz cavolo nero
2 tbsp extra virgin olive oil
1 small onion, finely chopped
1 tbsp tomato purée
approx. 650 ml/1¼ pints hot vegetable stock
1 x 400g/14 oz tin of borlotti beans
100 g/3½ oz quick-cook polenta
grated Parmesan cheese, to serve

First prepare the cavolo nero. Remove and discard the hard stems, then roughly chop the leaves and set aside.

In a medium-sized saucepan, place the olive oil over a medium heat and sweat the onion, then stir in the chopped cavolo nero. In a jug, stir the tomato purée into 550 ml/19 fl oz hot stock, then add to the pan and bring to the boil. Cover with a lid, reduce the heat and cook for about 20 minutes until the cavolo nero is tender.

Stir in the borlotti beans with their liquid and gently cook for a couple of minutes. Pour in the remaining hot stock (100 ml/3½ fl oz) and gradually add the polenta, stirring continuously with a wooden spoon for about 3–5 minutes (check the instructions on the packet for precise cooking times). If you find the soup too thick, simply add more hot stock.

Serve immediately in bowls with a generous sprinkling of freshly grated Parmesan.

Cooking Note
At the end of cooking, if you find the soup a little too thick, simply add more hot stock. It will thicken as it cools and, if you have any leftovers, you can literally cut the mixture into slices and either fry or bake.

Islands 87

GATHULIS

Cheesy potato fritters

This ancient recipe comes from an inland region of Sardinia known as Ogliastra where, in a few of the towns and villages, they are known as *orrubiolu*. Traditionally, they were made with a local cheese called *casu fisciu* and fried in pork fat for a crispier finish. However, these days vegetable or sunflower oil is an acceptable and healthier alternative. The fritters were once served as a main meal, but these days they are delicious enjoyed as an *aperitivo* alongside some olives, cured meats and a crisp cold glass of sparkling or white wine.

MAKES APPROX. 25

300 g/10½ oz potatoes, peeled and cut into chunks

200 g/7 oz durum wheat semolina flour (semola rimacinata), plus extra for dusting

75 g/2¾ oz feta cheese, grated

50 g/1¾ oz Pecorino cheese, grated

1 tbsp extra virgin olive oil

1 tsp sea salt

vegetable or sunflower oil, for frying

Cook the potatoes in a pan of boiling salted water until tender, then drain and allow to steam-dry – they have to be very dry so they don't exude any moisture. Mash and combine with the flour, cheeses, olive oil and salt and mix well to obtain a soft dough.

On a lightly floured surface, take small pieces of the dough and roll out each one into a thin sausage shape, approx. 18 x 1 cm (7 x ½ inches), then close and seal the two ends together to make an oval shape.

In a deep and heavy-based pan, heat abundant frying oil and, when hot, add a few *gathulis* at a time. Deep-fry for 2–3 minutes on each side until golden brown, then transfer to kitchen paper to drain and serve warm with a fresh sprinkling of salt.

Ingredient Note
The local Sardinian cheese is not easily obtainable outside of the island so I have used a mix of feta and Pecorino as a substitute.

COUSCOUS TRAPANESE

Seafood couscous

This recipe is a legacy of the Arab invasions of Sicily in the 9th century and has been firmly rooted in the island's cuisine ever since, especially in the western coastal areas. North African couscous dishes tend to include meat, whereas this Sicilian version uses seafood. Don't be put off by the long list of ingredients. It's a really simple dish to prepare and makes for a wonderful Friday night fish supper. I had the pleasure of trying this dish while staying in the Sicilian port town of Trapani, where local fishermen sell the freshest of seafood every morning, directly from their brightly-coloured boats.

SERVES 4

For the fish stock
2 tbsp extra virgin olive oil
1 small onion, roughly chopped
1 small carrot, roughly chopped
3 anchovy fillets, roughly chopped
½ red chilli, finely chopped
2 bay leaves
1 tsp capers
2 small whole red mullets (approx. 275 g/9¾ oz)
1 small whole sea bass (approx. 165 g/5¾ oz)
1 small whole red snapper (approx. 125 g/4½ oz)
100 ml/3½ fl oz white wine
2 tsp tomato purée
700 ml/1¼ pints hot water
sea salt

For the shellfish
2 tbsp extra virgin olive oil
1 garlic clove, left whole and squashed
160 g/5¾ oz calamari, sliced, keep tentacles intact
4 large king prawns (150 g/5½ oz)
a splash of white wine

For the couscous
2 saffron strands
200 g/7 oz quick-cook couscous
2 cloves
pinch of ground cinnamon
zest of ½ lemon

Recipe continues overleaf

First make the fish stock. In a large saucepan, place the olive over a medium heat and sweat the onion, carrot, anchovy fillets, chilli, bay leaves and capers for a couple of minutes. Add all the fish and cook for about a minute on each side.

Increase the heat, pour in the white wine and allow to evaporate. In a jug, dilute the tomato purée with 700 ml/1¼ pints hot water, then pour into the pan and season with a little salt. Bring to the boil, then reduce the heat, cover with a lid and gently simmer for about 15–20 minutes until the fish is cooked through.

Carefully remove the fish, discarding the heads and bones, then set the fillets aside and keep warm. Pass the fish stock through a sieve and keep hot.

In a small bowl, dilute the saffron strands (for the couscous) in a little of the fish stock and set aside.

Now prepare the shellfish. Place the olive oil in a pan over a medium heat and sweat the garlic for a few seconds. Add the calamari, increase the heat a little and cook for about 4 minutes, turning every so often. Add the prawns and continue to cook for a couple of minutes. Add the white wine and allow to evaporate, continuing to cook for 2–3 minutes, until both the calamari and prawns are cooked.

In the meantime, prepare the couscous. Place the couscous in a heatproof bowl together with the cloves, cinnamon, saffron mixture and lemon zest and pour over 250 ml/9 fl oz of the hot fish stock, then cover and leave for about 5 minutes for the liquid to be absorbed – check the instructions on the packet for precise cooking times.

To serve, place the couscous in a large serving dish or divide between 4 individual plates. Top with the fish and shellfish and serve the remaining hot fish stock on the side with a ladle, so everyone can help themselves.

Ingredient Note
My version uses whole fish to make the stock, which are then filleted and eaten with the couscous along with the calamari and prawns. Alternatively, you could simply use raw fish heads for the stock and enjoy the finished dish with whatever shellfish you prefer.

SARDE A BECCAFICO

Filled baked sardines

The *beccafico* of this age-old Sicilian recipe title was a songbird that loved to feed on fruit. This gave their meat a deep, rich flavour and, considered a gourmet delicacy in the 18th century, they were hunted for the banquets of the Sicilian nobility and served stuffed with their own innards. The poor began to imitate this dish, using sardines instead of songbirds, which were plentiful and affordable, stuffing them with breadcrumbs and dried fruit. This dish is still very much alive and much loved, especially in the markets of Palermo.

SERVES 4–6

juice of 1 orange
2 tsp extra virgin olive oil, plus extra for greasing
3 tbsp runny honey
30 fresh sardines (approx. 600 g/1 lb 5 oz), butterflied with spines and heads removed
30 bay leaves
slices of 1 large orange, cut into quarters

For the breadcrumb filling
2 tbsp extra virgin olive oil
50 g/1¾ oz dried breadcrumbs
20 g/¾ oz raisins, soaked in a little lukewarm water
20 g/¾ oz pine kernels
30 g/1 oz caster sugar
handful of flat-leaf parsley, finely chopped
2 anchovy fillets, finely chopped
sea salt and freshly ground black pepper

Preheat the oven to 180°C Fan/200°C/400°F/gas mark 6.

In a small bowl, combine the orange juice, olive oil and honey and then set aside.

Now make the breadcrumb filling. In a small pan, place the olive oil over a medium heat and, when hot, lightly toast the breadcrumbs for a minute or so until the oil has been absorbed. Remove from the heat and place in a bowl.

Drain the raisins when softened, then place them on a chopping board with the pine kernels and finely chop. Add to the bowl with the breadcrumbs, along with the sugar, parsley and anchovy fillets and season.

Place the butterflied sardines, flesh-side up, on a board and place a little of the breadcrumb mixture in each, before rolling up (from the top of the head to the tail) and securing with a cocktail stick.

In a lightly oiled ovenproof dish, arrange the sardines tail-side up, making sure they are tightly packed, and tuck a bay leaf and orange slice quarter between each one. Pour the orange juice mixture over the top and bake in the oven for 25 minutes.

Remove from the oven, allow to rest for 5 minutes, then serve with a green salad and lots of fresh rustic bread.

Serving Suggestion
This can be served as an antipasto or as a main course with a green side salad and lots of rustic bread.

CONIGLIO ALL'ISCHITANA

Ischia-style rabbit

It seems strange that an island in the Mediterranean, situated across from the Bay of Naples, has rabbit as one of its signature dishes. However, the story goes that rabbits were brought to Ischia thousands of years ago by the Phoenicians and, thanks to their reproductive capabilities, the island has always had a plentiful supply. When the Siracusans invaded Ischia 2,000 years ago, the rabbit became their staple diet and has remained so over the centuries. In Ischia, the dish is cooked in a special terracotta pot and the local wild thyme, *pipernia*, is used for flavouring.

SERVES 4

- 1 x 1 kg/2 lb 4 oz whole rabbit (ask your butcher to cut it into chunks with bone)
- 400 ml/14 fl oz white wine
- 4 tbsp extra virgin olive oil
- 4 garlic cloves, left whole and squashed
- ½ red chilli, finely sliced
- handful of basil leaves, roughly torn
- 2 thyme sprigs
- 4 bay leaves
- 6 sage leaves
- 400 g/14 oz cherry tomatoes, halved
- handful of parsley, finely chopped, to garnish
- rustic bread, to serve
- sea salt and freshly ground black pepper

Place the rabbit in a dish, pour over 200 ml/7 fl oz of the white wine and leave to marinate for 10 minutes. Drain and pat dry the rabbit with kitchen paper.

In a pan, place the olive oil over a medium heat and sweat 2 garlic cloves with the chilli for about a minute to infuse the oil. Discard the garlic, then add the rabbit and seal well all over. Add the remaining white wine and cook for a minute.

Add the remaining garlic, the basil, thyme, bay, sage and cherry tomatoes and season with salt and pepper. Cover with a lid and cook over a gentle heat for about 50 minutes, until the rabbit is cooked through and tender.

Remove from the heat, sprinkle with the parsley to garnish.

Serving Suggestion

This is a very simple dish to prepare and is delicious served with rustic bread to mop up the juices.

FALSOMAGRO

Stuffed beef pot roast

There are many versions of this traditional Sicilian dish. Some argue that the name of the dish derives from the French *farce*, meaning stuffing, and the dish has foreign roots. However, it is more probable that it comes from the Italian that, literally translated, means 'false thin', as that is exactly what it is. On first appearances, it seems a perfectly innocent joint of beef, but then it reveals a surprise with a stuffing full of cured meats, minced meats and eggs. It is often cooked in a tomato sauce, but when I was served this dish in Palermo, in a Slow Food-recognized restaurant, it was cooked *in bianco,* meaning it simply had a light gravy, and it's this version that I have tried to recreate here.

SERVES 4

100 g/3½ oz minced beef
100 g/3½ oz minced pork
20 g/¾ oz grated Provolone picante cheese
10 g/¼ oz grated Parmesan cheese
10 g/¼ oz breadcrumbs
2 tbsp white wine
pinch of ground nutmeg
pinch of ground cinnamon
3 eggs
1 tbsp extra virgin olive oil
1 garlic clove, left whole and squashed
200 g/7 oz baby spinach leaves
500 g/1 lb 2 oz brisket or silverside beef, butterflied – ask your butcher to do this
40 g/1½ oz mortadella slices
sea salt and freshly ground black pepper

For the gravy

2 tbsp extra virgin olive oil
1 small onion, finely chopped
½ celery stalk, finely chopped
1 small carrot, finely chopped
1 litre/1¾ pints hot vegetable stock

Recipe continues overleaf

In a bowl, combine the minced meats, cheeses, breadcrumbs, white wine, nutmeg, cinnamon and 1 egg. Cover and place in the fridge.

In a frying pan, heat ½ tablespoon of olive oil, sweat the garlic for a minute, then discard. Stir in the spinach leaves, cook over a medium heat for a couple of minutes until wilted, then add some salt and pepper, remove from the heat and set aside.

In a small bowl, lightly beat the remaining 2 eggs with a little salt and pepper. Heat the remaining olive oil in a small frying pan, pour in a little of the egg mixture and cook to make a small omelette. Remove and set aside. Continue to making little omelettes until you have used up all the egg mixture – you should make about 2 or 3 depending on the size of your pan.

On a board or clean work surface, unroll the beef. Lay the slices of mortadella over it, then spread the minced meat mixture all over it, followed by the spinach and then top with the little omelettes – if necessary, slice the omelettes to make them fit. Carefully roll up the meat to enclose the filling and tie securely with kitchen string. Set aside.

For the gravy, in a pot large enough to accommodate the meat, heat the olive oil, then sweat the onion, celery and carrot over a medium heat for about 4 minutes until softened. Remove the vegetables and set aside. Add the meat to the pot and seal well all over. Pour in the stock, return the vegetables to the pan, cover with a lid and gently cook for 2¼ hours until the meat is cooked through. Depending on the size of the pot, you may need more stock so that the meat is more or less covered during cooking.

Remove the meat from the pot and place on a wooden board.

Increase the heat and cook the gravy for a couple of minutes until thickened slightly.

Slice the meat and serve with the gravy.

Serving Suggestion
Served with roast potatoes and greens, this makes a lovely Sunday roast. It can also be served cold the next day.

U CINU
POLLO RIPIENO E BOLLITO

Stuffed and boiled chicken

This old-fashioned dish from Ragusa in Sicily is traditionally made at the end of August to celebrate the feast of San Giovanni. The official feast day is 24 June, but because farmers were still working in the fields at that time, the feast was moved to the end of August when everyone was able to join in. It was traditional for rural families to make the dish using their own hen or cockerel, stuffing it to make it go further, and boiling it, to produce a broth that could be enjoyed as a first course with some small homemade pasta shapes.

SERVES 4

1 x 1.3 kg/3 lb boiling chicken (see Ingredient Note)
1 onion, quartered
1 celery stalk plus leaves, cut in half
1 carrot, left whole
2 cherry tomatoes, left whole
1 chicken stock pot or cube

For the stuffing
1 tbsp extra virgin olive oil
1 garlic clove, left whole and squashed
90 g/3¼ oz chicken giblets, roughly chopped
150 g/5½ oz minced beef
150 g/5½ oz minced pork
splash of white wine
80 g/2¾ oz bread, soaked in a little water
30 g/1 oz grated Parmesan cheese
1 egg
handful of flat-leaf parsley, finely chopped
sea salt and freshly ground black pepper

First make the stuffing. In a frying pan, place the olive oil over a medium heat and sweat the garlic for a minute or so, then discard. Add the chicken giblets and stir-fry for 2–3 minutes until cooked through, then remove and set aside. In the same pan, stir-fry the minced beef and pork to seal, then return the giblets to the pan with a splash of white wine and cook for about 3 minutes.

Remove the pan from the heat, transfer the contents to a bowl and set aside to cool. When cool, combine with the softened bread, the Parmesan, egg and parsley and season with some salt and pepper.

Fill the chicken cavity with this stuffing mixture and then fold the chicken skin over to ensure none of the filling escapes. Traditionally, cooks would sew the skin together, using a large needle and thread, but you could secure with several cocktail sticks instead.

In a large pot, place the stuffed chicken with the onion, celery, carrot and cherry tomatoes, cover with water and bring to the boil. Add the stock pot or cube, then partially cover with a lid and cook for about 3½ hours, until the chicken is cooked through. Check the pot and top up with hot water every now and again. If you are using a standard chicken, then only half the cooking time is required.

Carefully lift the chicken out of the broth and transfer to a board for carving. Strain the broth through a sieve and either serve as a first course with some cooked *pastina* (small pasta shapes), or reserve for another time (cool, then refrigerate for up to 3 days).

Slice the chicken and serve immediately with the vegetables.

Ingredient Note
Ask your butcher for a boiling chicken (usually an older hen) or cockerel, which are the best options for this dish as they result in a delicious rich-tasting broth.

SA COCCOI PRENA

Sardinian bread rolls filled with potato, cheese and mint

This age-old bake from the rural Ogliastra area in Sardinia, made with simple local ingredients, provided the ideal packed lunch for shepherds who were away all day herding their sheep. The nutritious filling, encased in a homemade bread dough, is the same as for the Sardinian filled pasta *culurzones*, which comes from the same area. They make a delicious snack or are delicous served with an aperitif.

MAKES APPROX. 14

For the dough
1 x 6g/⅛ oz fresh yeast
200 ml/7 fl oz lukewarm water
300 g/10½ oz 00 flour, plus extra for dusting
2½ tsp sea salt

For the filling
750 g/1 lb 10 oz potatoes, peeled and cut into chunks
100 g/3½ oz grated Pecorino cheese
1 garlic clove, finely chopped
½ handful of mint leaves, finely chopped
sea salt and freshly ground black pepper

First make the bread dough. Dilute the fresh yeast in a little of the lukewarm water. In a bowl or stand mixer, combine the flour and salt, add the yeast mixture and gradually add enough of the remaining lukewarm water to obtain a dough. Knead for 5 minutes, then form into a ball, cover with a cloth and leave to rest in a warm place for 2 hours, or until doubled in size.

In the meantime, prepare the filling. Boil and mash the potatoes, stir in the grated Pecorino, the garlic and mint, then season with salt and pepper to taste. Set aside.

Preheat the oven to 160°C Fan/180°C/350°F/gas mark 4.

On a lightly floured work surface, roll out the dough as thin as you can and, using a 10-cm/4-inch round cookie cutter, cut out circles.

Take a circle in one of your palms and place a dollop of the filling in the centre, then fold all the edges up to enclose it and pinch together in a few places. A little of the filling will still be visible but don't worry, that's fine. Repeat until you have used up all the filling and dough.

Line a flat baking tray with baking paper and arrange the filled dough pieces on top, then bake for 25 minutes until golden.

Remove the bread rolls from the oven, leave to rest for about 5 minutes, then enjoy hot or cold.

PANE SQUARATO

Aniseed bread

Bread is sacred all over Italy, but in Salemi in Western Sicily, it's also an artform, often worked into shapes depicting animals, fish, plants and religious figures; traditionally given to the church or the poor on annual feast days. There is even a museum in the town to showcase the elaborate sculptures. This particular bagel-type bread from Marsala was traditionally made during Easter to represent the crown of Jesus. The name *squarato* means 'parboiled' as it is boiled before baking, resulting in a smoother, shinier crust.

MAKES 4 LARGE ROLLS

4 g/⅛ oz fresh yeast

approx. 230 ml/8¼ fl oz lukewarm water

400 g/14 oz durum wheat semolina flour (semola rimacinata), plus extra for dusting

6 g/⅛ oz sea salt

1 tsp aniseed seeds

½ tsp olive oil

Dilute the yeast in a little of the lukewarm water. Then, in a large bowl, combine the flour, salt, aniseed and yeast mixture before gradually adding enough of the remaining lukewarm water to obtain a dough. Knead for 10 minutes to form a ball, then cover with a cloth and leave to rise in a warm place for 1 hour, or until doubled in size.

Divide the dough into 4 pieces of approx. 110–120 g/3¾–4¼ oz each, leaving about 70 g/2½ oz (to be used for the garnish).

Take one of the larger pieces of dough and, on a lightly floured work surface, roll out to an approximate length of 30 cm/12 inches. Close the ends into a circle, then repeat with the three remaining large pieces of dough.

Roll out the small piece of dough as thin as you can, then cut out 16 flower shapes. Dampen with water to stick, then place 4 on each roll. Cover with a cloth and set aside to rest for 1 hour. Preheat the oven to 220°C Fan/240°C/475°F/gas mark 9.

Add the olive oil to a large pot of salted water and bring to the boil. Immerse each bread roll, one at a time, into the boiling water and cook for 10-15 seconds. Drain and leave to dry on a board dusted with flour for about 10 minutes until cool.

Line a flat baking tray with baking paper and arrange the bread rolls on it. Bake for 10 minutes, then reduce the oven temperature to 200°C Fan/220°C/425°F/gas mark 7 and continue to bake for a further 20 minutes until golden.

Equipment Note
You will need a small flower-shaped cookie cutter.

PANE FRATTAU

Sardinian bread bake with tomato and poached eggs

This Sardinian dish is made with the traditional crispy, wafer-thin bread known as *pane carasau* or *carta da musica*. It was invented by local rural farmers as a way of using up stale bread and making it go further with a handful of extra ingredients, like a simple tomato sauce and eggs, and makes a delicious meal at any time but especially for breakfast. You can make this either in one ovenproof dish or in individual terracotta ones.

SERVES 4

250 g/9 oz pane carasau
approx. 450 ml/16 fl oz hot vegetable stock
70 g/2½ oz grated Pecorino, plus extra for sprinkling
4 eggs

For the tomato sauce
3 tbsp extra virgin olive oil
1 large onion, finely chopped
800 ml/28 fl oz tomato passata
handful of basil leaves
sea salt and freshly ground black pepper

First make the tomato sauce. In a pan, place the olive oil over a medium heat and sweat the onion for about 4 minutes until softened. Add the tomato passata with a little water from rinsing out the jar or carton. Add the basil leaves and season with salt and pepper, then partially cover with a lid and gently simmer for about 25 minutes.

Preheat the oven to 180°C Fan/200°C/400°F/gas mark 6.

Break up the *pane carasau* into fairly big pieces, then place in a dish and pour over the vegetable stock to soften them for a few minutes.

Line an ovenproof dish with some of the tomato sauce, top with 2 layers of softened *pane carasau*, a layer of tomato sauce, a layer of grated Pecorino, then a double layer of *pane carasau* and continue making layers like these until you have finished all the ingredients, ending with grated Pecorino.

Bake in the oven for 15–20 minutes, or until the cheese has nicely melted.

Just before the end of cooking, poach the eggs, then place on top of the bake and serve immediately with a final sprinkling of grated cheese.

Ingredient Note
You can find *pane carasau* at Italian delis and online. The sell-by date is usually a long one and, as long as you store it correctly, it will last in your cupboard for a while. The crispy bread also makes a lovely light snack by itself and can be served with drinks or cured meats and cheese as an antipasto.

BACI PANTESCHI

Flower-shaped ricotta-filled pastries

From the remote and beautiful Sicilian island of Pantelleria come these pretty flower-shaped pastries that are filled with cinnamon-flavoured creamy ricotta and chocolate chips. Serve with a sweet dessert wine, such as Passito di Pantelleria, from the island.

MAKES 12

For the batter
150 g/5½ oz 00 flour, sifted
pinch of sea salt
1 egg, lightly beaten
200 ml/7 fl oz semi-skimmed or whole milk
abundant vegetable or sunflower oil, for frying

For the filling
500 g/1 lb 2 oz ricotta, well-drained
120 g/4¼ oz caster sugar
pinch of ground cinnamon
handful of chocolate chips
icing sugar, for dusting

In a large bowl, place the flour and salt, stir in the egg and gradually add the milk, whisking well to avoid any lumps, until you have a smooth batter-like mixture.

Heat abundant oil in a deep pan, immerse the flower mould into the hot oil quickly, then use tongs to transfer it to kitchen paper to drain.

Dip the top of the mould into the batter (do not immerse it completely or the flower shape will not come off when cooking) and then place straight into the hot oil, frying for about 30 seconds until golden and you have a flower pastry which slides out of the mould easily. Drain on kitchen paper. Repeat this process until you have used up all the batter.

In a bowl, combine the ricotta, sugar and cinnamon until it is nice and creamy, then place in a piping bag (or you can use a spoon). Arrange half the fried flowers on a serving plate and either pipe or spoon the creamy mixture on top. Scatter with a few chocolate chips, then lay a flower on top of each to create a sandwich, and press down gently.

Dust with a little icing sugar and serve immediately as these are best served warm.

Equipment Note
To make these, you will need to invest in a simple hand-held flower mould (see photo), readily available online.

GELO DI MELONE

Watermelon jelly

The origins of this Sicilian summer dessert are a little vague. Some believe it came about as a result of the Arab invasions of Sicily in the 9th century, while others believe it was introduced by the Arbëreshë, a population of Albanian origin that settled in the western part of the island, in the Palermo hinterland, from around the 14th century. However, regardless of its origins, this watermelon jelly is still available in the Palermo region of Sicily, where it is traditionally eaten on the feast day of Santa Rosalia in mid-July. It is very simple to make at home, especially during the summer when watermelons are in abundance, and the addition of pistachio nuts provides a lovely contrasting crunch.

SERVES 4

1 small watermelon (approx. 1.2 kg/2 lb 10 oz)
50 g/1¾ oz cornflour
60 g/2¼ oz caster sugar
20 g/¾ oz chocolate chips, plus extra to serve
a few pistachio nuts, chopped, to serve

Cut the watermelon in half, scoop out the flesh and discard the seeds. Place the flesh in a blender with its juices and whiz to obtain a smooth juice.

In a saucepan, combine the cornflour and sugar and gradually add the watermelon juice, whisking well. Place the pan over a medium heat and keep whisking until you obtain a custard-like consistency. Remove the pan from the heat and set aside to cool.

When cool, stir through the chocolate chips. Moisten the jelly mould and pour in the watermelon mixture. Cover with a plate and place in the fridge for about 4 hours until set.

Tip out onto a plate, sprinkle with more chocolate chips and the pistachio nuts and serve.

Equipment Note
You will need a 12-cm/4½-inch round silicone jelly mould to make this dessert.

GENOVESI DI MARIA GRAMMATICO

Custard-filled pastries

I was given this recipe by Maria Grammatico, whose pastry shop is located in the pretty hilltop village of Erice in Western Sicily. In her childhood, Maria was raised by nuns in the local orphanage. Times were hard and the nuns would bake cakes and make *Frutta Martorana* (beautiful fruit-shaped marzipan) to sell in order to make a living. The girls weren't given much of an academic education and were expected to help the nuns with their baking. Maria learned many skills and, when she came of age, she started to bake for the village and eventually opened up her own *pasticceria* (pastry shop). I had the pleasure to meet the lovely Maria, now well into her eighties but still very much involved in the business, when I visited Erice while researching this book. These delicious pastries are a favourite in her *pasticceria* and people come from all over the world to sample her beautiful sweet treats.

MAKES APPROX. 10 PASTRIES

For the pastry
125 g/4½ oz durum wheat semolina flour (semola rimacinata)
125 g/4½ oz 00 or plain flour, plus extra for dusting
125 g/4½ oz hard butter, cut into small pieces
100 g/3½ oz caster sugar
2 egg yolks
a little cold water
icing sugar, for dusting

For the filling
2 egg yolks
70 g/2½ oz caster sugar
zest of ½ lemon
250 ml/9 fl oz milk
20 g/¾ oz cornflour

First make the pastry. In a large bowl, combine the flours, add the butter and rub together with your fingertips until the mixture resembles fine breadcrumbs. Stir in the caster sugar, then gradually add the egg yolks with a little cold water to make a soft dough. Form into a ball and leave to rest for 30 minutes in the fridge.

Meanwhile, make the filling. In a small saucepan, combine the egg yolks and caster sugar and stir in the lemon zest. Mix a little of the milk with the cornflour to make a smooth paste and set aside, then gently heat the remaining milk in a separate saucepan. Stir the cornflour paste into the egg yolks, then place over a low heat and gradually whisk in the hot milk. Keep whisking for about 8 minutes until you obtain a thick, smooth custard. Remove from the heat, pour into a heatproof bowl, cover and set aside to cool.

Remove the pastry from the fridge and leave to rest for 5 minutes at room temperature. On a lightly floured work surface, roll out the pastry to a thickness of 5 mm/¼ inch – it might be easier to divide the pastry in two and work with each half separately.

Using a 10-cm/4-inch round cookie cutter, cut out about 20 circles and arrange half on a flat baking tray lined with baking paper. Place a dollop of the custard cream in the centre of each circle and brush around the edges with a little water.

Place another circle of dough over the top and press down well to secure the edges, so the filling doesn't escape during cooking. Bake at 150°C Fan/170°C/340°F/gas mark 3½ for 17–20 minutes until golden.

Remove from the oven, leave to cool slightly, then dust with sifted icing sugar and serve.

SU PISTEDDU DI SANT'ANTONIO

Honey pie

This sweet pie, which can be served warm or cold, is only really known in the mountainous Barbagia area of inland Sardinia, where traditions go back thousands of years. It was customary for housewives to decorate this to resemble an embroidered work of art, in honour of St Anthony Abate's feast in mid-January. It was made with a simple pastry of flour and lard and the filling was made with *vin cotto* – a grape juice cooked down to a thick, syrupy consistency. This was an ingredient most rural families had easy access to, especially if they made their own wine, but these days honey is widely used.

SERVES 8 (MAKES 1 PIE)

For the pastry
250 g/9 oz durum wheat semolina (semola rimacinata), plus extra to serve
½ x 8 g/¼ oz, oz sachet of Paneangeli (or 2 tsp baking powder)
50 g/1¾ oz hard butter, cut into small pieces
50 g/1¾ oz caster sugar
approx. 80 ml/2½ fl oz cold water

For the filling
250 ml/9 fl oz runny honey
zest of 1 orange
pinch of ground cinnamon
pinch of ground nutmeg
50 g/1¾ oz durum wheat semolina flour (semola rimacinata)

In a large bowl, mix the flour and baking powder. Add the butter and rub together with your fingertips until the mixture resembles fine breadcrumbs. Stir in the sugar and gradually add enough cold water (approx. 80 ml/2½ fl oz) to make a soft dough. Form into a ball, wrap in clingfilm, and leave to rest in the fridge while you prepare the filling.

Preheat the oven to 160°C Fan/180°C/350°F/gas mark 4.

In a small pan, place the honey, orange zest and spices and stir over a medium heat until the honey gently melts. As it begins to bubble, reduce the heat and gradually whisk in the flour, continuing to whisk over a low heat for about 4 minutes until the mixture turns into a jam-like consistency. Remove from the heat and set aside to cool.

Take the pastry, divide in half and roll out each half on a lightly floured work surface to a thickness of a pound coin. Cut out two 20 cm/8 inch circles (the easiest way is to place a bowl or plate of this size onto the pastry and cut around it with a pastry cutter).

Line a flat baking tray with baking paper and place one of the pastry circles on top. Tip the cooled filling into the centre and spread it evenly, leaving a little gap around the edge. Brush the edges with a little water.

Take the other pastry circle and, with the help of a skewer or thin piping bag nozzle, make patterns to resemble flower petals. Place the decorated circle over the filling and press to secure.

Bake in the oven for 20–25 minutes until golden.

PISTOCCHEDUS PRENU

Almond-filled pastries

These traditional Sardinian pastries are crispy, filled with an almond mixture and finished off with white icing. They take a little time and patience to make but, once made, they are beauties to look at and taste delicious too. You can choose a shape you prefer or make a variety and decorate how you like. They would make amazing wedding favours as well as Christmas tree decorations, or can be simply served on a plate with a tea or coffee.

MAKES APPROX. 30–35 PASTRIES

For the pastry

4 eggs

25 g/1 oz caster sugar

40 g/1½ oz butter or lard, softened at room temperature

zest of 1 lemon

400 g/14 oz 00 flour, plus extra for dusting

For the filling

150 g/5½ oz caster sugar

75 ml /2½ fl oz water

400 g/14 oz ground almonds

1 tsp orange flower water

1 dsp Cointreau or other orange-flavoured liqueur

For the icing

200 g/7 oz icing sugar

1 egg white

a few drops of lemon juice, if required

coloured sugar strands, silver balls, sugared flowers, for decoration

First make the pastry. In a large bowl, whisk the eggs and sugar until light and creamy, then whisk in the softened butter or lard and lemon zest. Gradually mix in the flour and work until you obtain a pastry consistency. Roll into a ball, wrap in clingfilm and leave to rest in the fridge for about 30 minutes.

In the meantime, make the filling. In a small pan, combine the sugar with 75 ml/2½ fl oz water and bring to the boil over a medium heat. Lower the heat and, stirring all the time, cook for a couple of minutes until the mixture begins to thicken.

Stir in the ground almonds, orange flower water and Cointreau and continue to cook over a low heat, stirring all the time, until the mixture becomes nice and thick. Remove from the heat, pour onto a plate and leave to cool.

Preheat the oven to 160°C Fan/180°C/350°F/gas mark 4.

Divide the dough into pieces (each approx. 100g/3½ oz) and, on a lightly floured surface, roll out each piece to get it as thin as you can – or use a pasta machine on its thinnest setting. Cut out rectangular pieces of thin pastry, each about 12 x 8 cm/4½ x 3¼ inches. Spread a blob of filling over the pastry rectangle, then roll up from the long side to enclose the filling, sealing the edges well with a little water.

From here, you can shape this cigar into a ring or horse-hoof shape or a little sausage or an S shape, or whatever shape you like. Line a flat baking tray with baking paper and arrange the pastries on top, then bake in the oven for 20 minutes until lightly golden.

In the meantime, sift the icing sugar into a bowl, gently whisk the egg white and add to the icing sugar, mixing well to obtain a fairly dense glaze. If necessary, add a drop or two of lemon juice, but be careful as you don't want the glaze to be too watery.

Remove the pastries from the oven and set them aside until they are cool enough to handle. Decrease the oven temperature to as low as it can go. Take each pastry and dip the top into the glaze, then return to the baking tray and sprinkle the coloured sugar strands or silver balls or sugared flowers over the top. Place the tray back in the oven for about 4 minutes to harden the glaze, then remove and leave to dry out for a couple of hours.

Storage Note
Stored in an airtight container, these pastries will keep for at least a week.

NORTH

The diverse landscape of Northern Italy, with its mountains, lakes, coasts and plains, has produced a varied and robust culinary tradition that provides a nice contrast to the Mediterranean flavours of Southern Italian cuisine. Polenta and rice are the staples here, rather than pasta. Butter is used instead of olive oil and cow's milk cheeses are plentiful – fontina, mascarpone, Parmesan, Asiago, Gorgonzola, dolcelatte, Taleggio and Montasio, to name just a few. Steaming platefuls of hearty dumplings are popular in the mountain towns and villages, as are *pizzoccheri* (a type of buckwheat pasta) and hearty soups featuring potatoes and cabbage. Beef and game dishes are common and *bresaola*, air-dried beef, is a popular cold cut.

The North has two of the richest regions of Italy – Lombardia and Emilia-Romagna. The capital of the former, Milan, is the Italian centre of business and fashion, and Bologna, the capital of Emilia-Romagna, is known as *la grassa* ('the fat one') for the bounty of food its region produces – ragù Bolognese, mortadella, balsamic vinegar, egg-based pastas like lasagne, tagliatelle and tortellini, and of course Italy's crowning glories, Parmesan cheese and prosciutto.

Polenta, a northern staple of *cucina povera* dates back to Roman times. Initially made from ancient grains, such as barley, broad beans, spelt, rye or buckwheat, polenta evolved after corn was introduced from the 'New World' in the 1500s. Northern Italy's climate proved ideal for corn cultivation and polenta soon became a staple for the poor, who would often eat it like porridge – perhaps adding a little milk, if available, for extra nutrition. Wealthier families would add butter, cheese, or even serve it with a vegetable or meat stew. There is an Italian saying: '*La polenta e' utile per quattro cose – serve da minestra, serve da pane, sazia e scalda le mani*', which means 'Polenta is useful for four things – good as a soup, used as bread, it's filling and warms your hands'. Until Italy's post-war economic boom in the 1950s and 1960s, polenta was often the primary food for poor rural families, leading to the nickname *polentoni* (polenta eaters) for Northern Italians. However, over time, this cornmeal staple has been embraced all over Italy and is now often served as a gourmet food in high-end restaurants.

Rice is also a staple ingredient of Northern Italy where the paddy fields of the Po and Venetian plains produce abundant quantities. It arrived in Europe via Asia and it's said the Romans used it for medicinal and cosmetic purposes. According to historians, it wasn't until the 15th century that rice cultivation began in Italy and was found to be an excellent staple, especially in times of famine. Some historians believe that rice was introduced by the Arabs and was consumed in Sicily as early as the 9th century; which probably explains why *arancini* (rice balls) are a popular Sicilian street food. During this period, large platters of saffron-infused rice with meat and vegetables were commonly shared on a table and people would take rice, meat and vegetables in their hand and roll it before eating. Over time, this evolved into the risotto rice ball filled with meat ragù, cheese or vegetables, which is so loved as a snack in Sicily and throughout Italy to this day.

The earliest recorded area of rice cultivation in Italy was around the 1480s in the Pisa area, which spread further north to Lombardy, where favourable conditions were ideal for rice production. Over time, this spread to the plains of Piemonte and to southern Veneto, areas which are now the highest producers of rice in Europe. Typically rice was always boiled, but in 1809, the first risotto recipe appeared in a cookbook where the grain was sautéed in butter together with onion and sausage, with saffron added before being cooked in a broth. This recipe evolved to become the classic *Risotto alla Milanese*; now so loved in Milan and surrounding areas that it is often cooked on a daily basis in families as well as served as an accompaniment to dishes like *Ossobuco* (braised veal shanks).

During the middle ages, Northern tribes introduced butter to the region and, in the cool mountain regions with their herds of cows, this was absorbed seamlessly into the local cuisine. In fact, in Northern Italy, butter and cheesy sauces are far more common than the olive oil and tomato-based sauces that are so stereotypically Italian. In Italy, a frequent joke is that the country can be divided in two, between butter in the north and olive oil in the central and southern regions.

However, the northern coastal regions depart somewhat from this trend. The rocky coastline of Liguria and its abundance of sweet-smelling basil and olive trees align this region with Mediterranean flavours and, if you've ever been to the Cinque Terre, you could easily mistake it for the Amalfi Coast with its pretty hilltop villages, impressive cliffs plunging into the sea and its relatively mild weather even in winter months. The food is somewhat lighter compared to other northern regions, with lots of fish and seafood dishes taking centre stage and delicate basil pesto coating *trofie* pasta.

In the northeast, the Venice lagoon brings an abundance of fish and seafood and this, combined with northern staples, characterizes its cuisine. Dishes like squid ink risotto, scampi with polenta or *sarde in saor* (sweet and sour sardines) are classics of the region.

The freshwater fish of Northern Italy's three wonderful lakes – Como, Maggiore and Garda – also bring a distinctive flavour to local cuisine. Lake Como boasts an unusual dish of *missoltini*, which are local fish that have been salted and dried. The tradition dates to a time before refrigeration, but these are still a speciality of the area. Lake Garda's microclimate produces lemons, not what you would expect in the north, but the small highly-prized citrus fruit is a delicacy. Used in the local cuisine to enhance fish dishes, risotto, desserts and ice cream, it's also made into a delicious liqueur, *limoncino*.

There are regions in Northern Italy which border several countries – Austria, Slovenia, France and Switzerland. The mountainous region of Trentino Aldo-Adige, covering a large part of the Dolomites, borders Austria and Switzerland and comprises of two provinces, Aldo Adige (or Sud Tirol) in the north and Trentino in the south. From the early 1800s, this region was part of the Austrian-Hungarian Empire until 1919 when it was returned to Italy. During the reigns of Mussolini and Hitler in the 1930s, it was agreed that the German-speaking population was to be transferred to Germany and, with great difficulties, returned to their homes after the war. It is no wonder then that about a third of the population of Trentino Alto Adige speak German as their first language. This obviously impacted the culture of the region and, of course, the cuisine which comprises both Italian and German influence. Hearty mountain dishes are the norm, with meat stews served alongside polenta and gnocchi as well as dishes of sausage and sauerkraut. One of the most traditional dishes is *Canderli*, also known as Austrian *Knodeln*; these dumplings are made from stale bread, eggs, milk and flour and often flavoured with speck, a local smoked cured ham. *Spatzle* is a regional pasta made with flour and eggs, then pushed through a colander or potato masher creating small spherical shapes. For dessert, apple *strudel* is a classic here, as well as *krapfen* (doughnuts) and *buchteln* (see page 158).

Friuli-Venezia Giulia is a region bordering Austria to the north, Slovenia to the east and Venice to the west. In 1815, Friuli belonged to the Kingdom of Lombardy-Venice, while Trieste (now the region's capital) and Gorizia were part of Austria, and later the Austrian-Hungarian Empire, until 1919 when it was returned to Italy. Throughout history, the region's neighbours all made their mark on the area claiming it theirs at some point. Although Italian is the official language, Friulian, Slovene and German are also spoken. So, the region is a mix of Venetian, Slavic and Germanic influences on culture, customs and naturally the food. As in most other northern territories, polenta is a staple which, here, is often served with *Goulasch*, a rich beef stew flavoured with paprika, influenced by eastern Europe. *Cjalsons* (see page 138) are a type of filled pasta with the Slavic sweet and savoury flavour *avjar*, a Balkan-inspired smoky sauce made with peppers and aubergines which makes a good accompaniment to cold and cured meats. San Daniele prosciutto, made in the village of the same name, has become a world-wide delicacy alongside *blecs*, a fresh pasta made with white and buckwheat flour which resembles small handkerchiefs.

The regions of Piemonte and Valle d'Aosta in northwest Italy both border France and Switzerland. Piemonte, which literally translates to 'at the foot of the mountain', is one of Italy's wealthiest regions with Turin as its capital. North of Piemonte is Italy's smallest region, Valle d'Aosta, nestled in the Alpine valley and home to the majestic high peaks of Monte Bianco (Mont Blanc) and Monte Rosa. From about the 10th century, parts of both these areas were ruled by the House of Savoy, Italy's royal family. France occupied this territory on and off until the unification of Italy in 1861, when parts of Savoy, including Nice, were given to France. These areas are now known as Savoie and Haute-Savoie. The French language was widely spoken in both Piemonte and Valle d'Aosta, however, over the years this has declined. Valle d'Aosta still retains French as an important language, but the majority of the population are bilingual and fluent in Italian, too.

The proximity of France and French rule over history has certainly made its mark in both culture and the kitchen of both regions. French sophistication entered Piemontese cuisine through both the ingredients and dish presentation. The shining star of this area is the luxurious white truffle which commands exorbitant prices. French influence is reflected throughout a lot of Piemontese dishes, especially sauces like *Bagna Cauda* – a garlic and anchovy dip served with crudités – or *Bagnet Vert* (salsa verde), a green sauce made with parsley, gherkins and capers to go with boiled meats. Risotto is the main staple here, producing some of the best rice for traditional dishes like *Panissa*, a risotto made with local frogs. *Vitel Tonne* (vitello tonnato) is a classic dish of thin slices of veal smothered in a rich tuna and caper sauce. For dessert, *Bonet* (a type of French-inspired crème caramel) or *Marrons Glacés* (candied chestnuts) are served.

In the mountainous Valle d'Aosta, dishes tend to be heavier and *Fonduta alla Valdostana*, a savoury, melty cheese fondue, is popular. *Carbonnade Valdostana*, a rich beef stew cooked in red wine with herbs and spices, makes a hearty main. And there's *Zuppa alla Valpellinense* (see page 141), a thick soup of bread, weighty cheese and cabbage.

BAZOTTI ROMAGNOLI

Baked capelli d'angelo pasta

This unusual recipe originated in the rural area of Valle del Savio in Emilia Romagna, where *Bazotti* was made for special occasions. Handmade *tagliolini* pasta (like tagliatelle but thinner) was placed in a broth of pork bones to soften, then transferred to a dish over an open fire with the addition of pork fat, cheese and breadcrumbs, resulting in a dish resembling a baked pasta. My version is really simple to make as it places all the ingredients, including the raw pasta, in an ovenproof dish to bake until the stock has been absorbed and you get a nice crunchy topping. It's delicious served with a fresh mixed salad.

SERVES 4

80 g/2¾ oz butter, plus extra for greasing
250 g/9 oz egg capelli d'angelo pasta
freshly ground black pepper
100 g/3½ oz grated Parmesan cheese
500 ml/18 fl oz vegetable stock
1 tbsp breadcrumbs
mixed salad, to serve

Preheat the oven to 180°C Fan/200°C/400°F/gas mark 6 and grease a 20-cm/8-inch square ovenproof dish with a little butter.

Place half the *capelli d'angelo* in the greased dish and dot with half the butter, then sprinkle with black pepper and half the grated Parmesan. Make another layer like this one and then pour in the vegetable stock.

Scatter the breadcrumbs over the top, then bake in the oven for about 20 minutes until all the liquid has been absorbed and the top is golden brown. If the top isn't golden, place under a hot grill for a couple of minutes to colour.

Leave to rest for a few minutes, then serve with a mixed salad.

PASTICCIO DI PASTA ALLA FERRARESE

Pasta pie

This pasta pie from Ferrara in Emilia Romagna was a popular dish at noble banquets during Renaissance times. According to *Pellegrino Artusi's* recipe in his book *Science in the Kitchen and the Art of Eating Well* (1891), the filling was mainly made from offal, like sweetbreads and chicken giblets, as well as dried mushrooms and truffles. The recipe is also mentioned in *Tomaso di Lampedusa's* classic 1958 novel, *Il Gattopardo* (The Leopard), which shows just how widespread this recipe had become at the time. Traditionally made in a copper pie dish, it was often made to celebrate *Carnevale,* just before the Lenten period when meat was forbidden. It does take a little time to prepare, but your efforts will certainly be rewarded. Serve with a mixed-coloured leaf side salad.

SERVES 6

300 g/10½ oz tortiglioni pasta or rigatoni or broken-up ziti

1 small egg yolk, beaten with a little milk, for egg wash

For the pastry

330 g/11½ oz 00 flour, plus extra for dusting

pinch of sea salt

180 g/6¼ oz hard butter, cut into small pieces, plus extra for greasing

60 g/2¼ oz caster sugar

zest of ½ lemon

3 egg yolks, lightly beaten

For the ragù

2 tbsp extra virgin olive oil

½ small onion, finely chopped

½ celery stalk, finely chopped

½ small carrot, finely chopped

2 bay leaves

100 g/3½ oz minced beef

100 g/3½ oz minced turkey or chicken

Grease a 24-cm/9½-inch round pie dish or cake tin with butter and dust with flour, then set aside.

Now make the pastry. In a large bowl, place the flour, salt and butter and rub together with your fingertips until the mixture resembles breadcrumbs, then stir in the sugar and lemon zest. Gradually add the egg yolks and, if necessary, a little cold water until it comes together to make a smooth dough. Form into a ball, then divide into two pieces, making one piece a little bigger.

On a lightly floured work surface, roll out the larger piece of dough – approx. 3 mm/⅛ inch thick – and use it to line the prepared dish/tin. Take the other piece of dough and roll it out to a similar thickness and into a circle approx. 24 cm/9½ inch in diameter. Place between 2 sheets of baking paper and place both the dish/tin and baking paper in the fridge to rest.

In the meantime, prepare the ragù. In a frying pan, heat the olive oil and sweat the onion, celery, carrot and bay leaves for about 5 minutes until softened. Add the minced meats and crumbled sausages and cook over a medium heat until sealed.

Add the mushrooms, season with salt and pepper and stir-fry for a minute or so. Increase the heat, add the white wine and cook for a minute, then lower the heat, cover with a lid and cook for about 25 minutes until the meat is nicely browned.

Recipe continues overleaf

2 Italian pork sausages, skin removed (approx. 150 g/5½ oz in total)

200 g/7 oz chestnut or button mushrooms, finely sliced

80 ml/2½ fl oz white wine

sea salt and freshly ground black pepper

For the béchamel sauce

25 g/1 oz butter

25 g/1 oz 00 flour

300 ml/10 fl oz milk

pinch of ground nutmeg

20 g/¾ oz grated Parmesan cheese

sea salt and freshly ground black pepper

Preheat the oven to 150°C Fan/170°C/340°F/gas mark 3½.

Now make the béchamel sauce. In a small, non-stick saucepan, melt the butter over a medium heat, then take off the heat and whisk in the flour. Add a little milk and whisk until you obtain a smooth paste, then return the pan to the heat and gradually add the remaining milk, whisking all the time over a medium heat until the mixture thickens slightly. Remove from the heat, season with salt and pepper and a pinch of nutmeg and stir through the grated Parmesan.

Bring a large pot of salted water to the boil and cook the pasta for just half of the time stated on the packet, then drain well. Stir the ragù into the béchamel sauce, add the parcooked pasta and stir again to combine.

Take the chilled pastry out of the fridge. Fill the lined dish/tin with the pasta, ragù and béchamel mixture, then cover with the pastry lid, crimping the edges together to seal. With any pastry trimmings, cut out pretty shapes to garnish on top, if you like. Brush with egg wash and bake in the oven for 50–55 minutes until golden brown.

Remove from the oven, leave to rest for 5 minutes, then carefully remove from the dish/tin, slice and serve immediately.

Recipe Note
This pie is different to many other Italian savoury pies as it uses a sweet shortcrust pastry, which adds contrast to the savoury filling. It sounds strange but you have to try it as it really does work. Or if you prefer, simply omit the sugar to make a savoury pastry.

GNOCCHI ALLA VENEZIANA

Baked Venetian-style gnocchi

Gnocchi have been made since medieval times. The original recipe used only flour and water and it was centuries later, after potatoes had been introduced to Italy in the 16th century, that gnocchi started to resemble what we know today.

This recipe is similar to an ancient Venetian recipe, which was traditionally eaten sprinkled with cinnamon and raisins. I have adapted it with butter and Parmesan for a simple dish made with everyday storecupboard ingredients.

SERVES 2

50 g/1¾ oz butter
250 ml/9 fl oz milk
200 g/7 oz 00 flour
pinch of ground nutmeg
pinch of sea salt
a little vegetable oil for greasing
35 g/1¼ oz grated Parmesan cheese
mixed salad, to serve (optional)

Preheat the oven to 180°C Fan/200°C/400°F/gas mark 6. Take about 10 g/¼ oz of the butter and grease a 20-cm/8-inch square or round ovenproof dish; set aside.

Place the milk and 15 g/½ oz of the butter in a non-stick saucepan over a medium heat and bring to the boil.

Reduce the heat before whisking in the flour, nutmeg and a pinch of salt until combined. Remove from the heat and tip the mixture onto a lightly oiled work surface and wait a few minutes until the mixture cools a little. Once cool enough to handle, gently knead until the mixture comes together into a soft dough.

Using a rolling pin, roll out the dough to a depth of 1 cm/½ inch. Using a 4-cm/1½-inch round cookie cutter, cut out your gnocchi. Knead and roll out the offcuts until you have used up all the dough.

Bring a large pan of salted water to the boil, then drop in the gnocchi, a few at a time, and cook until they rise to the top. Remove with a spider utensil, then place on a lightly oiled board or tray to cool slightly. Place the gnocchi in the buttered ovenproof dish, slightly overlapping each other. Dot with the rest of the butter and sprinkle with the grated Parmesan.

Bake in the oven for 25 minutes until golden before removing and leaving to rest for 5 minutes.

Cooking Note
Ensure you whisk the mixture well to avoid lumps from forming; if they do, use an electric whisk.

LASAGNE MEDIEVALI CON LE NOCI

Walnut lasagne

Lasagne can be traced back to the Ancient Greeks and Romans, who would make dishes from layered ingredients with a type of pasta known as *lagana*. During the Middle Ages, this evolved into a dish we are more familiar with today, although it was still very basic and not the rich baked pasta dish we are used to. A simple pasta dough was made with flour and water, rolled out into sheets and cooked in a meat stock, it was then layered on a plate with whatever ingredients were available. For example, a popular version was with walnuts and spices. I have also used walnuts here, as well as ricotta and Parmesan for a lighter version of lasagne, which can be served for lunch or dinner with a green salad on the side.

SERVES 4

approx. 1.5 litres/2¾ pints beef or chicken stock
olive oil, for greasing and drizzling
500 g/1 lb 2 oz ricotta
50 g/1¾ oz grated Parmesan cheese
pinch of ground cinnamon
2 cloves, very finely crushed
60 g/2¼ oz walnuts, very finely chopped
green salad, to serve
sea salt and freshly ground black pepper

For the pasta sheets
200 g/7 oz 00 flour, plus extra for dusting
110 ml/3¾ fl oz lukewarm beef or chicken stock

First make the pasta. In a large bowl, place the flour and gradually add the lukewarm stock, combining until you obtain a smooth dough. Knead for a couple of minutes, then shape into a ball, cover with a cloth and set aside to rest for 30 minutes.

Take the dough and divide into 4 portions. On a lightly floured surface, roll out each portion of the dough to about 3 mm/⅛ inch thick – or use the no. 2 setting on a pasta machine.

Cut the pasta sheets into rectangles approx. 15 x 8 cm/6 x 3¼ inches (similar to lasagne sheets). They don't have to be exact and it doesn't matter if you get rectangles or squares or both.

Preheat the oven to 200°C Fan/220°C/425°F/gas mark 7.

In a large pot, bring the beef or chicken stock to the boil, then plunge in a few lasagne sheets at a time until they float to the top (this will only take a few seconds). Using a spider utensil, carefully transfer the cooked pasta to a lightly oiled tray.

In a bowl, combine the ricotta with 40 g/1½ oz grated Parmesan, a pinch of salt and a couple of tablespoons of the stock, then set aside.

In another small bowl, combine the cinnamon, cloves and some black pepper, and set aside.

Lightly grease a 20-cm/8-inch square ovenproof dish with some oil. Place a layer of the pasta sheets on the base, followed by a layer of the ricotta mixture, a pinch of the spice mixture, a sprinkling of walnuts and a drizzle of olive oil. Cover with a layer of pasta sheets and repeat with the other layers, until you finish with lasagne sheets and the remaining grated Parmesan.

Add a couple of tablespoons of the stock around the side of the dish, then cover with foil and bake in the oven for 30 minutes.

Remove the foil and bake for a further 10 minutes until the top is golden. Leave to rest for a couple of minutes, then serve with a fresh green salad.

Cooking Note
As the lasagne sheets are cooked in stock, I also use a little stock to make the fresh pasta. It's the same as using water but with just a slight hint of extra flavour.

CJALSONS

Sweet 'n' savoury ravioli

This pasta, with an unusual sweet and savoury filling, comes from the Friuli area in north-east Italy and is a good example of how Italian food has been influenced by its Austrian neighbour. *Cjalsons* have a more Central European flavour than other Italian filled pasta dishes and some say their origin is linked to merchants bringing spices and other exotic ingredients from Venice to Germanic countries, hence the cinnamon and nutmeg in the filling. Prunes, apples or local greens and herbs are also often used and the sweetness combines well with the saltier cheese and breadcrumb topping. I warn you though – they are very filling!

SERVES 4
(MAKES APPROX. 34)

For the dough
250 g/9 oz 00 flour, plus extra for dusting
1 egg, lightly beaten
approx. 85 ml/3 fl oz cold water

For the filling
100 g/3½ oz potatoes, boiled
3 dried figs (approx. 50 g/1¾ oz), finely chopped
25 g/1 oz plain rich tea-type biscuits, finely crumbled
25 g/1 oz raisins, softened in a little water, then drained
pinch of ground nutmeg
pinch of sea salt
½ tsp ground cinnamon
½ tbsp cocoa powder

For the topping
120 g/4¼ oz butter, melted
15 g/½ oz breadcrumbs, lightly toasted
grated Parmesan cheese, for sprinkling (optional)

First make the pasta. Place the flour in a large bowl or on a clean work surface, make a well in the centre, add the egg and gradually add approx. 85 ml/3 fl oz cold water, mixing to make a smooth dough. Form into a ball and leave to rest for 30 minutes.

In the meantime, make the filling. In a bowl, lightly mash the boiled potatoes and combine with the rest of the filling ingredients, then set aside.

On a lightly floured surface, roll out the pastry to about 5 mm/¼ inch thick – or use the no. 2 setting on a pasta machine. Using an 8-cm/3¼-inch round cookie cutter, cut out circles and place small dollops of the filling mixture in the centre of each. Brush the edges with a little water, then fold over to make half-moon shapes and press together to seal.

Bring a large pot of salted water to the boil, drop in the *cjalsons*, a few at a time, and cook for about 4–5 minutes. Remove using a spider utensil or slotted spoon and transfer to a large serving dish or divide between 4 individual plates. Top with the melted butter and sprinkle with the breadcrumbs, and, some grated Parmesan, if desired.

ZUCCHINI ALL'AMARETTI

Courgettes with amaretti

Cooking with crunchy amaretti biscuits is quite popular in the northern regions of Lombardy and Emilia Romagna. For example, the classic *Tortelli di Zucca* usually combines pumpkin and amaretti biscuits – and is delicious. And *Zucchine alla Visconti*, which dates back to Renaissance times, fills courgettes with a mixture of béchamel sauce, cream, mascarpone, raisins and amaretti biscuits and is delicious but also very rich. My version uses simpler ingredients, and the addition of Parma ham provides a nice saltiness that contrasts really well with the sweetness of the amaretti. Serve with a mixed salad and some rustic bread.

SERVES 2–4

- 2 x medium-large-sized courgettes (approx. 280 g/ 10 oz each)
- 20 g/¾ oz butter, plus extra for greasing and dotting
- 1 garlic clove, crushed and left whole
- 60 g/2¼ oz grated Parmesan cheese
- 6 slices of Parma ham (approx. 90 g/3¼ oz), finely chopped
- 30 g/1 oz amaretti biscuits, crumbled
- handful of flat-leaf parsley, finely chopped
- handful of breadcrumbs
- mixed salad, to serve
- rustic bread, to serve
- sea salt and freshly ground black pepper

Preheat the oven to 180°C Fan/200°C/400°F/gas mark 6.

Slice the courgettes in half lengthways and scoop out the flesh to create hollow 'boats'. Chop the flesh and set aside.

In a small frying pan, melt the butter and sweat the garlic for a minute, then add the chopped courgette flesh with a little salt and cook for about 5 minutes. Remove from the heat, discard the garlic and allow to cool a little.

Stir through the Parmesan, Parma ham, crumbled amaretti and parsley and season with a little pepper. Fill the courgette 'boats' with this mixture.

Place the filled courgette 'boats' in a lightly buttered ovenproof dish, sprinkle with the breadcrumbs and dot with some butter. Cover with foil and bake for 30 minutes, then remove the foil and continue to bake for 15 minutes until golden.

Remove from the oven and serve either hot or cold with a mixed salad and some rustic bread.

SEUPA A LA VAPELENENTSE (ZUPPA ALLA VALPELLINESE)

Cheesy cabbage bake

Although the Italian title suggests a soup, this dish is actually more of a bake, or at least my version is. Originating in the village of Valpelline in the Alpine region of Valle d'Aosta, it is simply made from local ingredients – cabbage, fontina cheese and leftover bread – and was designed to provide the locals with much-needed nutrition and calories, in order to survive the harsh, cold mountainous winters.

SERVES 4

1 medium-sized Savoy cabbage (approx. 600 g/1 lb 5 oz cleaned weight)

70 g/2½ oz butter, plus extra for greasing

30 g/1 oz pancetta, very finely chopped

pinch of sea salt

400 g/14 oz bread, sliced

280 g/10 oz fontina cheese, half cut into cubes and half thinly sliced

280 ml/9½ fl oz hot vegetable stock

Preheat the oven to 180°C Fan/200°C/400°F/gas mark 6 and lightly butter a cake tin or ovenproof dish approx. 30 x 20 cm/ 12 x 8 inches.

Using a sharp knife, remove the tough outer leaves and hard interior core of the cabbage and discard. Roughly chop the leaves and set aside.

In a pan, melt the butter over a medium heat and cook the pancetta for a couple of minutes until crispy, then stir in the cabbage with a pinch of salt, cover with a lid and cook for about 15 minutes, until the cabbage has softened.

Line the prepared cake tin or ovenproof dish with the sliced bread. Add a layer of half the cabbage and scatter with the cubed cheese, then add another layer of the remaining cabbage and finish off with the slices of cheese. Pour over the hot stock and then bake in the oven for 25 minutes until the cheese has nicely melted and turned golden brown.

Remove from the oven, leave to rest for a couple of minutes and then serve.

Ingredient Note
If you can't get fontina cheese, a good mature Cheddar is perfect.

BRANDACUJIN

Creamy salt cod

Salt cod, or *baccalà* in Italian, is a popular preserved fish eaten in many Mediterranean countries. Each coastal area in Italy has its own version and this recipe comes from the north-western Liguria region. In the *cucina povera* tradition, in times before refrigeration, fish was often dried or preserved in salt as a way of keeping it for longer, and sailors would take it with them on long voyages. In local dialect, *brandacujin* refers to the Italian *brandare,* meaning 'to shake or toss', and refers to the point in the method where you shake the pan to make the dish nice and creamy.

SERVES 4

400 g/14 oz salt cod

240 g/8½ oz potatoes, peeled and cut into chunks

6 tbsp extra virgin olive oil

2 garlic cloves, minced

handful of flat-leaf parsley, finely chopped, plus extra for garnish

zest of 1 lemon, plus juice to serve

4 slices of rustic bread, lightly toasted, to serve

a few Taggiasca olives, to serve

sea salt and freshly ground black pepper

Soak the salt cod in cold water for at least 12 hours or overnight, changing the water a couple of times, and then drain.

In a pan, place the salt cod with the potatoes, cover with fresh water and bring to the boil over a medium heat. Skim off any foam that collects on the surface and cook for about 20 minutes, until both the fish and potatoes are cooked through. The fish should be nice and flaky.

Drain, then mash the potatoes, and then mash the fish with a fork and combine with the mashed potatoes. Set aside.

In a pan, place 3 tablespoons of olive oil and sweat the garlic for a minute to infuse the oil. Add the mashed fish and potato mixture and stir-fry over a medium heat until all the oil has been absorbed. Stir in the parsley, lemon zest and remaining olive oil and season with salt and pepper. Give the pan a shake and continue cooking like this for a couple of minutes – shaking the pan until you obtain a creamy consistency.

Serve on slices of toasted bread with a sprinkling of fresh parsley on top, a squeeze of lemon juice and some Taggiasca olives on the side.

Serving Suggestion

This is delicious served on slices of toasted rustic bread for an antipasto or to serve with drinks.

TROTA COMASCA

Trout fillets with anchovy sauce

The Northern Italian lakes are full of wonderful fish like pike, tench, eel, lavaret, perch and, of course, trout, and in Italian cooking, they are often preserved and marinated. On Lake Como, a popular way was to put them in salt and dry them out, known as *missoltini*. In the past, it was not uncommon to see rows of fish drying out in the sun, but nowadays, they are industrially dried out in ovens and sold in vacuum packs. Marinated freshwater fish known as *al carpione* are pickled with the flavours of finely chopped vegetables, olive oil and lemon juice, and this is the method I've chosen here. As trout is easily obtainable, I marinated it first to remove any traces of the muddy taste that is so often found in freshwater fish. Baked and served with a tangy anchovy butter sauce, it is delicious served with some steamed new potatoes and greens.

SERVES 4

4 trout fillets, weighing 125 g/4½ oz each, skin on
4 tbsp extra virgin olive oil
juice of 2 lemons
1 small red onion, roughly chopped
a couple of rosemary sprigs
sea salt
steamed new potatoes, to serve
steamed greens, to serve

For the sauce
50 g/1¾ oz butter
4 anchovy fillets, very finely chopped
1 large garlic clove, finely diced
100 ml/3½ fl oz white wine
handful of flat-leaf parsley, very finely chopped

Place the trout fillets in a dish.

In a jug, combine the olive oil, lemon juice, onion and rosemary with a little salt and then pour the mixture over the trout fillets to cover. Set aside to marinate at room temperature for 30 minutes.

Preheat the oven to 200°C Fan/220°C/425°F/gas mark 7.

Line a flat baking tray with baking paper and place the marinated trout fillets (with the marinade) on the baking tray, then bake in the oven for 10 minutes until cooked through.

In the meantime, make the sauce. In a small pan, melt the butter with the anchovy fillets, garlic and a little salt over a medium heat, then pour in the wine, increase the heat a little and, stirring from time to time, cook until the wine evaporates and the sauce reduces. Stir in the parsley.

Remove the trout fillets from the oven and transfer to serving plates. Pour over the sauce and serve immediately with steamed new potatoes and greens.

BRUSCITTI DI BUSTO ARSIZIO

Slow-cooked beef

This recipe was given to me by my wife, Liz. Her Nonna was from the town of Busto Arsizio in Lombardy and she would often make this type of beef stew – cooking lesser cuts of meat for a long time along with a little fennel from the fields to give the meat aroma. I was a little sceptical and didn't think the recipe would work without the traditional *soffritto* method (cooking onion, carrot and celery in olive oil until soft and brown) and sealing the meat, but I was pleasantly surprised. The secret is to cut the beef into small pieces but not to mince it, and to cook it very gently for a long time as this way the meat cooks in its juices.

SERVES 4

1 kg/2 lb 4 oz mixed beef cuts like chuck (braising) steak, beef shank and skirt

1 garlic clove, peeled and left whole

2 tsp fennel seeds

40 g/1½ oz butter, cut into small pieces

30 g/1 oz pancetta or lardo (pork fat), very finely chopped

100 ml/3½ fl oz red wine

polenta or mashed potatoes, to serve

sea salt and freshly ground black pepper

Remove any excess fat from the beef with a sharp knife and cut the meat into tiny pieces. Set aside.

Place the garlic clove and fennel seeds in a small muslin sachet and tie securely so nothing can escape.

In a heavy-based pot (cast-iron is ideal), place the beef, butter, pancetta or *lardo* and muslin sachet and season with salt and pepper. Cover with a tight-fitting lid, place over a low heat and leave to cook very gently for 2½ hours, checking from time to time. You will find that the meat exudes liquid and will cook in these juices.

After 2½ hours, ensure the meat is cooked through, then increase the heat to medium, remove the lid, pour in the wine and cook for about 8 minutes, until most of the wine has evaporated but you still have a sauce.

Remove the muslin sachet and discard, then serve with either polenta or mashed potatoes.

Serving Suggestion
This stew is traditionally served with runny polenta, but I also like it with creamy mash, along with a nice glass of red wine – I like Nebbiolo but any full-bodied red would work well.

DULS IN BRUSC

Sweet and sour chicken liver sauce

This old, traditional recipe from the Lombardy region dates to a time when all rural families kept chickens in their backyard and, as nothing was ever wasted, would use the liver to make a sweet and sour pâté-type sauce like this one. In fact, in the local dialect, the name of this dish literally translates as 'sweet and sour'. I often enjoy this as a snack, spread on lightly toasted bread, but if you have leftover roasted or boiled chicken, this makes a wonderful tangy accompaniment. Once made, keep covered in the fridge for up to 3 days.

SERVES 4

6 eggs
80 g/2¾ oz chicken livers, roughly chopped
4 anchovy fillets, finely chopped
2 tbsp capers, finely chopped
4 tbsp extra virgin olive oil
1 tbsp lemon juice
2 tbsp white wine vinegar
4 slices of rustic bread, to serve

Bring a pot of water to the boil and cook the eggs until hard-boiled – about 10 minutes. Before the end of cooking, add the chicken livers to the boiling water and cook for about 5 minutes until cooked through, then drain.

Transfer the livers to a chopping board and finely chop, then set aside. Leave the eggs to cool, then peel and remove the egg whites.

Place the egg yolks in a bowl and squash them with a fork, then add the anchovy fillets, capers and chopped livers. Gradually whisk in the olive oil to make a smooth paste, then whisk in the lemon juice and white wine vinegar.

Lightly toast the bread and spread the mixture over the top, or serve as an accompaniment to cold chicken.

Ingredient Notes
These days, chickens are generally not sold with their giblets, so you will need to buy the livers separately. Any good butcher will have them. I like to chop the leftover egg whites and use them as a simple sandwich filling.

ZUPPA IMPERIALE

Semolina cubes in meat broth

In this delicious but curious soup from Emilia Romagna, a mixture of semolina, eggs, butter and Parmesan is baked and then cut into small cubes, which are then served with a hot meat broth, a little like croutons. Although very simple to make, it would have been very expensive for ordinary people in the early 1800s and so was reserved for special occasions among the nobility, hence the name, which translates as 'imperial soup'. There is also a similar version made in Cremona in Lombardy, which is locally known as *Zuppa di Pasta Reale*.

SERVES 4

140 g/5 fl oz semolina
4 eggs, lightly beaten
80 g/2¾ oz butter, melted
90 g/3¼ oz grated Parmesan cheese
pinch of sea salt
pinch of ground nutmeg
1.5 litres/2¾ pints meat stock

Preheat the oven to 160°C Fan/180°C/350°F/gas mark 4.

In a bowl, combine the semolina, eggs, melted butter, grated Parmesan, salt and nutmeg and whisk well to a smooth consistency, avoiding any lumps.

Line a baking tray (30 x 22 cm/12 x 8½ inches) with baking paper and pour in the mixture, levelling out the surface with a spatula, then bake in the oven for 30 minutes until risen and golden.

Remove from the oven and leave to rest for a couple of minutes, then tip the baked polenta out onto a board and remove the baking paper. Cut into approx. 1-cm/½-inch squares, then set aside.

In a large pan, heat the meat broth until piping hot. Divide the semolina squares between 4 individual soup bowls, then pour over the hot broth and serve immediately.

Ingredient Note
If you are making a *bollito* (see page 102), either with chicken or beef, then the broth would be ideal to use in this recipe. Alternatively, you can use a stock cube or stock pot to make the broth and, if you prefer, you can use a vegetable one.

FRITTO MISTO MODERNO ALLA MILANESE

Mini Milanese mixed fry

In Italian cooking, and especially in *cucina povera*, no part of any ingredient was ever wasted, and so a traditional Milanese *fritto misto* comprised of veal parts, such as brain, sweetbreads, lungs, kidneys, livers and other innards, as well as some vegetables, and everything was coated in breadcrumbs and fried. However, these days, the dish is in decline as this type of meat is no longer so in favour with the younger generation. When I'm in Northern Italy, I love a *fritto misto*, but have also scaled back and often include only calves' liver (like this recipe), which is easily obtainable from the butcher, along with mushrooms and courgettes. Place everything on a large serving platter in the middle of the table and get everyone to tuck in.

SERVES 4

400 g/14 oz calves' liver

4 tbsp extra virgin olive oil

small handful of sage leaves, very finely chopped

plain flour, for dusting

abundant breadcrumbs (approx. 300g/10½ oz), for coating

6 eggs, beaten with a pinch of sea salt

2 medium-sized courgettes, cut in half and sliced lengthways into thick batons

200 g/7 oz chestnut mushrooms, cleaned and thickly sliced or left whole if small button ones

120 g/4¼ oz butter

abundant vegetable or sunflower oil, for frying

lemon wedges, to serve

sea salt and freshly ground black pepper

Place the calves' liver in a dish with the olive oil and sage. Season with salt and pepper and set aside to marinate for at least 10 minutes.

Meanwhile, prepare the vegetables. Place the flour and breadcrumbs on two individual plates, and place the beaten egg in a wide, shallow bowl. Take each vegetable piece and dust each in flour, then dip into beaten egg and roll to coat in the breadcrumbs. Set aside.

Remove the liver from the marinade and coat each piece in flour, then egg, then breadcrumbs, like the vegetable pieces.

In a large, deep-sided frying pan, heat the butter with abundant vegetable oil over a medium heat until hot. Add the mushrooms to the oil and cook for 2–3 minutes until golden, then remove using a spider utensil or slotted spoon and drain on kitchen paper and keep warm. Add the courgettes and cook for a minute or so until golden, then drain on kitchen paper and keep warm.

Add the calves' liver and cook for 3–4 minutes on each side until golden and crispy. Transfer to kitchen paper to drain.

Serve the *fritto misto* immediately with lemon wedges on the side, for squeezing over.

PANISCIA

Bean and sausage risotto

This traditional rural recipe from Novara in the Piemontese region has age-old roots and is believed to have been made even before rice was cultivated in the area, using ancient grains such as barley, rye, oatmeal or millet. It uses a soft salami known as *salami della duja* but, as this is not widely available outside of the region, I have used Italian pork sausage which, combined with cavolo nero and borlotti beans, makes for a very tasty and nutritious risotto. Serve with a glass of red wine such as Barolo or any type of full-bodied red.

SERVES 4

- *2 tbsp extra virgin olive oil*
- *70 g/2½ oz butter*
- *60 g/2¼ oz pancetta, finely chopped*
- *2 shallots, finely chopped*
- *160 g/5¾ oz Italian pork sausages, skin removed and crumbled*
- *240 g/8½ oz cavolo nero, stems discarded and thinly sliced*
- *300 g/10½ oz arborio rice*
- *100 ml/3½ fl oz red wine*
- *2 x 400g/14 oz tins of borlotti beans, drained but reserve the liquid*
- *approx. 1.5 litres/2¾ pints hot vegetable stock*
- *60 g/2¼ oz grated Parmesan cheese, plus extra to serve (optional)*

In a wide pan, place the olive oil with 30 g/1 oz of butter over a medium heat, add the pancetta, shallots, sausage meat and cavolo nero and sweat for about 5 minutes, until the shallots are softened and the sausage meat is coloured.

Stir in the rice until each grain is coated in the fat, then add the red wine and allow it to evaporate. Add the bean liquid with a ladle of the hot stock and cook over a low-medium heat, stirring, until absorbed. Continue to add the hot stock gradually and keep cooking for about 15 minutes. When the rice is cooked 'al dente', stir in the borlotti beans.

Remove the pan from the heat and gently mix in the remaining butter and the grated Parmesan. Serve with an extra dsting of grated Parmesan, if desired.

UCCELLINI SCAPPATI ALLA CREMONESE

Pork rolls

There are various ways of making this dish from the region of Lombardy in Northern Italy. The name literally translates to 'birds which have escaped' and refers to the ancient practice of barbecuing game birds or, when these were not available, other pieces of meat. This recipe was given to me by my friend Paolo who comes from Cremona and it involves cooking the pork rolls in a *pistaada*, a mixture of pork fat, garlic and parsley. It's a rich dish but so delicious. Although traditionally served with polenta, I like it with lots of rustic bread to mop up the sauce and with a green side salad for freshness.

SERVES 4

8 slices of pancetta (approx. 130 g/4¾ oz in total)
8 thin slices of pork loin (approx. 600 g/1 lb 5 oz in total)
8 large sage leaves
60g/2¼ oz lardo (pork fat), very finely chopped
2 garlic cloves, finely chopped
handful of flat-leaf parsley, very finely chopped
3 tbsp extra virgin olive oil
200 ml/7 fl oz white wine
1 tbsp tomato purée
500 ml/18 fl oz hot vegetable stock
rustic bread, to serve
green side salad, to serve
sea salt and freshly ground black pepper

Place the pancetta slices on a flat board and lay the pork slices on top, season with salt and pepper and place a sage leaf in the centre of each, then roll up into a sausage shape and secure with a cocktail stick. Set aside.

In a bowl, combine the chopped *lardo* with the garlic and parsley.

In a pan, large enough to accommodate all the pork rolls, place the olive oil and sweat the *lardo* mixture over a medium heat for 30 seconds. Add the pork rolls and seal on all sides, then increase the heat, pour in the white wine and allow it to evaporate, while basting the meat with the juices.

In a jug, combine the tomato purée with the hot stock, then pour into the pan. Reduce the heat, partially cover with a lid, then gently cook for 50 minutes, until the meat is cooked through and the liquid has reduced to a gravy-like consistency.

Remove from the heat and serve with rusti bread and a green side salad.

Ingredient Note
Try to get good *lardo* (pork fat) from a local Italian deli.

MICON AD PAN AD RIS (PANINI AL RISO)

Rice bread rolls

This rice bread recipe comes from the fertile plains of Pavia, in south-western Lombardy, Northern Italy, where rice fields dominate the landscape. From the 19th century, this land was worked by the *mondine*; groups of women who spent backbreaking hours knee-deep in water under the hot sun, preparing the land for rice to be cultivated. However, these women not only played an important role in rice farming, but also became a collective political voice during the early 20th century, campaigning for women's rights and better working conditions and combating fascism during WW2.

MAKES 13

1 litre/1¾ pints water
50 g/1¾ oz arborio rice
20 g/¾ oz fresh yeast
500 g/1 lb 2 oz strong white bread flour, plus extra for dusting
250 g/9 oz rice flour
1¼ tbsp extra virgin olive oil
pinch of sea salt

In a large saucepan, bring 1 litre/1¾ pints water to the boil and drop in the rice. Reduce the heat slightly and simmer for about 20 minutes, until the rice is cooked through and soft. Drain, reserving the cooking water, and set aside to cool until lukewarm.

In a bowl, combine about 200 ml/7 fl oz of the lukewarm cooking water with the yeast, stirring until it dissolves.

In a separate large bowl, combine both flours, then add the yeast mixture, olive oil and the cooked rice with a pinch of salt and gradually add enough of the remaining cooled cooking water to make a dough. If you find you need more liquid, add a little lukewarm water. Knead the dough for about 10 minutes, then cover with a cloth and leave to rise in a warm place for 2 hours.

Take the dough and divide it into 13 pieces (approx. 100 g/3½ oz each), then roll out each piece into an 18 cm/7 inch length, cut into three strands and braid together as you would if plaiting hair. Or, you can simply roll each piece into a round shape.

Place the bread rolls onto a lightly floured baking tray, cover with a cloth and leave to rest in a warm place for 1 hour.

Preheat the oven to 180°C Fan/200°C/400°F/gas mark 6. Bake the bread rolls for 20–25 minutes until golden on top. Set aside to cool a little, then serve while still warm.

BUCHTELN

Filled brioche

This 'tear and share' brioche cake is a popular sweet treat from the Aldo Adige / South Tyrol area of Northern Italy and is a typical example of how the cuisine of this region has been influenced by its border neighbour, Austria. It takes a little time to prepare but is very simple to make and is really worth the wait. Delicious filled with a good-quality apricot jam, I like to serve it still warm for a teatime treat.

MAKES 14

150 g/5½ oz 0 flour or strong white bread flour, plus extra for dusting
150 g/5½ oz 00 flour
4 g/⅛ oz easy-blend dried yeast
45 g/1½ oz caster sugar
4 tbsp milk, plus extra for glazing
2 eggs
50 g/1¾ oz butter, melted
1 tbsp rum
1 tsp vanilla extract
⅓ tsp sea salt
zest of 1 lemon
14 tsp apricot jam
icing sugar, for dusting

In a bowl or stand mixer, combine the flours, dried yeast and caster sugar. In a smaller bowl or jug, gently whisk together the milk, eggs, melted butter, rum, vanilla extract, salt and lemon zest and gradually add this to the dry ingredients, mixing well to form a soft, slightly sticky dough. Form into a ball, cover with a cloth and leave to rise in a warm place for about 2 hours.

Line a 20-cm/8-inch round cake tin with baking paper.

Place the dough on a lightly floured work surface and divide into 14 pieces, weighing approx. 35–40 g/1¼–1½ oz each. Roll each piece into a small ball and, using a rolling pin, flatten them into small circles. Place a teaspoon of apricot jam in the centre of each and close the edges well to form small balls and enclose the jam. Arrange the dough balls, seam-side down, in the prepared tin, cover with a cloth and leave to rest for 1 hour.

Preheat the oven to 160°C Fan/180°C/350°F/gas mark 4.

Brush the dough balls with a little milk to glaze and then bake in the oven for 25 minutes, until golden brown.

Remove from the oven and leave to cool slightly in the tin, then remove and dust with a little icing sugar. Serve by 'tearing and sharing'.

TORTA POLENTA E OSEI

Sponge, hazelnut cream and marzipan cake

The title of this cake means 'polenta and birds' and comes from a time when game birds were regularly hunted for cooking and often served on a plate of hot steaming polenta. However, this is a sweet cake covered with yellow marzipan and chocolate-coated birds and comes from Bergamo, an alpine region in Northern Italy, where, in the early 1900s, it was created to showcase the excellent pastry chefs of the town. Between the two world wars, the cake declined in popularity, but during the post-war boom of the 1950s and 1960s, it became everyone's favourite Sunday treat. For me, it is always a fantastic and truly delicious celebration cake.

SERVES 10–12

For the sponge
- 5 eggs
- 170 g/6 oz caster sugar
- 1 tbsp runny honey
- 220 g/8 oz butter, melted, plus extra for greasing
- 150 g/5½ oz 00 flour, plus extra for dusting
- 100 g/3½ oz fecola di patate (potato flour)
- 1 x 16g/½ oz sachet of Paneangeli or 3½ tsp baking powder
- pinch of sea salt

For the buttercream meringue
- 200 g/7 oz butter, softened
- 40 g/1½ oz hazelnut cream
- 2 tbsp rum
- 3 egg whites
- 170 g/6 oz icing sugar, sifted

Preheat the oven to 150°C Fan/170°C/340°F/gas mark 3½. Grease a 22 cm/8½ inch hemisphere cake tin with butter and dust with flour, then set aside.

First make the sponge. In a bowl or stand mixer, whisk the eggs, caster sugar and honey for about 10 minutes until light, fluffy and paler in colour. Gradually whisk in the melted butter – if you are using a stand mixer, switch to a low setting. Gently fold in the flours with the Paneangeli and a pinch of salt until well combined, then pour the mixture into the prepared tin and level the surface. Bake for 55 minutes until springy to the touch and golden. Insert a thin skewer through the middle and, if it comes out clean, the sponge is cooked.

Remove from the oven and leave to cool completely in the tin.

In the meantime, make the buttercream meringue. In a bowl, place the butter and hazelnut cream and, using an electric hand whisk, whisk until nice and creamy. Whisk in the rum and then set aside.

In another clean bowl, whisk the egg whites and icing sugar for a couple of minutes until well combined. Place the bowl over a bain-marie and continue whisking with an electric hand whisk for a few minutes until the mixture has thickened and you can stand a teaspoon up in it.

Recipe continues overleaf

For the drizzle

50 ml/3¼ tbsp Alchermes liqueur
100 ml/3½ fl oz water
30 g/1 oz caster sugar

icing sugar, for dusting
400 g/14 oz marzipan
approx. 50 g/1¾ oz dark chocolate, chopped
20 g/¾ oz piece of candied cedro (citron), cut into thin strips, for decoration

Remove the bowl from the bain-marie and leave to cool completely. Gradually beat the buttercream into the meringue mixture. If you find the mixture too runny, place it in the fridge for about 30–60 minutes to thicken. The consistency should be spreadable and you need enough to fill and cover the cake.

Now prepare the drizzle. In a small saucepan, place the Alchermes liqueur, 100 ml/3½ fl oz water and the sugar over a medium heat and stir until the sugar has dissolved. Remove from the heat and set aside to cool.

When the sponge has cooled completely, carefully remove it from the tin and evenly slice across twice so that you end up with three layers of sponge. Place the bottom slice on a serving plate or cake board, brush it with a little of the drizzle, then spread some buttercream meringue mixture over and sandwich with the middle slice on top. Layer as before with the drizzle and some buttercream meringue. Now take the top sponge slice and brush all over with the drizzle, then place on top to create the final layer, and cover the cake all over with the remaining buttercream meringue.

On a surface lightly dusted with icing sugar, roll out the marzipan as thin as you can and carefully cover the whole cake with it, then trim it to fit.

Re-roll the marzipan trimmings and model little birds with it (see photo on page 161). Over a bain-marie, melt the dark chocolate and then coat the marzipan birds with it. Leave to dry before arranging over the top of the cake with the candied cedro.

Place the decorated cake in the fridge for at least a couple of hours before serving.

Storage Note

I like to make this cake the day before as this allows time for the flavours of the buttercream meringue and drizzle to infuse the sponge perfectly. It will keep in the fridge for up to 3 days.

Ingredient Notes

Alchermes is a red Italian liqueur, infused with spices. It's known for its subtle aroma and is commonly used in Italian cakes and desserts. You can use black modelling icing to make the blackbirds (instead of using the marzipan trimmings for making these) and this will eliminate the need to dip them in melted chocolate. Use any leftover marzipan for extra detailing, if you like.

FRITTELLE DI POLENTA

Sweet polenta fritters

There are many versions of sweet fritters these days, made with fruit, filled with creamy mixtures, nutella, ricotta and so much more. However, the traditional ones come from the Veneto area, where they have always been popular. As far back as the 1600s, tradespeople known as the *fritoleri* were dedicated to making and frying fritters and would pass their skills down the generations. Made with flour in Venice and polenta in Verona, they were especially enjoyed during carnival time just before Lent.

MAKES APPROX. 22

380 ml/13 fl oz water
100 g/3½ oz quick-cook polenta
15 g/½ oz caster sugar, plus extra for coating
25 g/1 oz self-raising flour
1 small egg, lightly beaten
75 g/2¾ oz raisins, soaked in 2 tbsp Marsala wine
zest of ½ lemon
pinch of sea salt
abundant vegetable or sunflower oil, for frying

First make the polenta. Bring 380 ml/13 fl oz water to the boil in a non-stick saucepan and gradually add the polenta, whisking well over a low-medium heat for about 5 minutes (check the instructions on the packet for precise cooking times).

Remove the pan from the heat and set aside to cool. When cool, add the sugar, flour, egg, Marsala-soaked raisins, lemon zest and a pinch of salt and mix well together. If the consistency seems a bit too liquid, add a little more flour.

Heat abundant oil in a deep-sided pan over a medium-high heat until hot. Using 2 tablespoons, shape the polenta mixture into quenelles and deep-fry batches in the oil for about 4 minutes until golden.

Remove using a spider utensil or slotted spoon, drain well on kitchen paper and, while still hot, coat the fritters in sugar. Serve immediately.

DOLCE CERTOSINO

Fruit and honey cake

This ancient cake, traditionally eaten at Christmas in Bologna, is not really known outside of the town. It is said to have been made in medieval times by the Certosini monks, hence its name, with the pretty glazed decoration on top resembling stained-glass windows in churches. However, in the late 1800s, a famous baker of the town created a version with rich, fancy ingredients that was almost certainly intended for the nobility. As it is rich, a small slice per person will suffice, but it will keep so it's perfect to make during the festive period as a change from English Christmas cake, or if you want something richer than the classic Italian Panettone.

SERVES 12

butter, for greasing
300 g/10½ oz 00 flour, sifted, plus extra for dusting
150 g/5½ oz candied/glacé fruit
280 ml/9½ fl oz runny honey
45 g/1½ oz cocoa powder
1 x 16g/½ oz sachet of Paneangeli or 3½ tsp baking powder
1 tsp ground cinnamon
40 g/1½ oz walnuts, roughly chopped
250 g/9 oz dark chocolate, grated
180 g/6¼ oz whole blanched almonds
200 g/7 oz quince or apple jam
150 ml/5 fl oz Marsala wine
1 tsp caster sugar

Preheat the oven to 140°C Fan/160°C/325°F/gas mark 3. Grease a 24-cm/9½-inch savarin cake tin with butter and dust with flour (or you can simply use a normal round cake tin and place an aluminium dariole mould in the centre).

Finely chop half of the candied/glacé fruit into small cubes. In a small saucepan, place 250 ml/1 cup/9 fl oz of the honey over a low heat and gently heat through, then add the chopped candied fruit and mix together well. Remove from the heat and set aside.

In a large bowl, combine the measured flour, the cocoa powder, Paneangeli, cinnamon, walnuts, chocolate and 150 g/5½ oz of the almonds. Stir in the jam and Marsala wine, along with the candied/glacé fruit and honey mixture and mix well to incorporate all the ingredients. The mixture will be quite dense and almost dough-like.

Recipe continues overleaf

Fill the prepared cake tin with the mixture, level the surface and set aside.

In a small saucepan, place the sugar and a dessertspoon of the remaining honey, add the remaining almonds and caramelize over a low heat for about 3 minutes.

Finely slice the remaining candied/glacé fruit and arrange decoratively over the top of the cake along with the caramelized almonds.

Bake the cake in the oven for 45 minutes, until a skewer comes out clean.

Remove the cake from the oven. In a small pan, heat the remaining honey and brush all over the top of the cake as a glaze, then set aside to cool completely in the tin.

Carefully turn the cake out of the tin onto a board or plate and serve. Alternatively, if stored in an airtight tin or container, it should keep for at least a week.

Cooking Note
It's best to make the cake a few days or a week in advance to allow all the flavours to infuse.

Ingredient Note
The cake needs a colourful variety of good-quality candied/glacé fruit, like orange, lemon, cedro and red and green cherries. I also like to use whole peel, which tends to be better quality, and you can slice it the way you like.

SOUTH

As we head to Southern Italy, food and culture begins to look very different. The region is also known as the *Mezzogiorno,* meaning 'midday' or 'noon', when the sun is at its highest, and its hot climate means the pace of life is slower, longer lunches are the norm, landscapes are wilder, and the sea is warm and welcoming.

The regions that comprise Southern Italy are Molise, Campania, Puglia, Calabria and Basilicata. Each one is blessed with mountainous landscapes, miles of beautiful coastline and rich food traditions, and all three are loved by those who live there with an intense pride. Regional food specialities are celebrated each year with festivals and the culture is kept very much alive, in contrast to some of the bigger towns in the North, where customs have been lost over the years. The coastal waters provide abundant seafood and the freshest of fish, while inland, sheep and goats supply meat and dairy products. In the Campania region, water buffalo are reared for their unique milk that is essential in the production of mozzarella cheese, which has become an indispensable ingredient in every Italian kitchen.

There's an old Neapolitan saying: '*Chist' è o paese do sole*', meaning 'This is the land of the sun'. The long, hot, dry summers bring endless hours of sunshine and the warm climate delivers an abundance of wonderful produce, especially the beloved tomato. Towards the end of summer, it is not unusual to see people in villages across the South bottling their own tomatoes or laying them out to dry in the hot sun. Some of the best varieties come from the volcanic soils of Vesuvius and their plentiful supply has influenced many of the most popular dishes in Southern Italian cooking, and beyond. Pizza, for example, was born in Naples and began as a type of street food. When tomatoes first arrived from the 'New World', the nobility viewed them with suspicion as possibly poisonous, so they were taken up by the poor. At the start of the day, bakers would test the temperature of their ovens with flat pieces of dough and these flatbreads, layered with tomato, were sold on the street to the poor. In the late 1800s, a famous baker made one for Queen Margherita with tomato, mozzarella and basil, and the modern-day pizza was born. In fact, Naples had a thriving street food scene throughout the 19th century and stalls serving seafood dishes, like fish stews and hot octopus broth, were very common, as well as *Cuoppo di Pesce*, a paper cone filled with delicious fried seafood, which you can still find today.

Historically, Southern Italy was poor compared to the North and people created dishes out of whatever was available to them. Neapolitans were known as *mangiafoglie* or 'leaf eaters' because their diet mainly consisted of vegetables and greens, and it wasn't until the 1700s that Naples and the surrounding area began to produce its own pasta. Made with flour and water, the pasta, known as *maccheroni*, was shaped into long strands and left to dry outside in the gentle breeze. It was then cooked in a large cauldron of boiling water, flavoured perhaps with a little animal fat and salt and, on a lucky day, served with a sprinkling of grated hard cheese, and this staple food became a lifesaver for the poor, who became known as the *mangiamaccheroni*. During the 1800s in Naples, tourists, rich merchants and aristocrats would often toss a few coins to the *lazzaroni* (street urchins) for the entertainment of watching them buy the pasta and stuff their faces by the fistful.

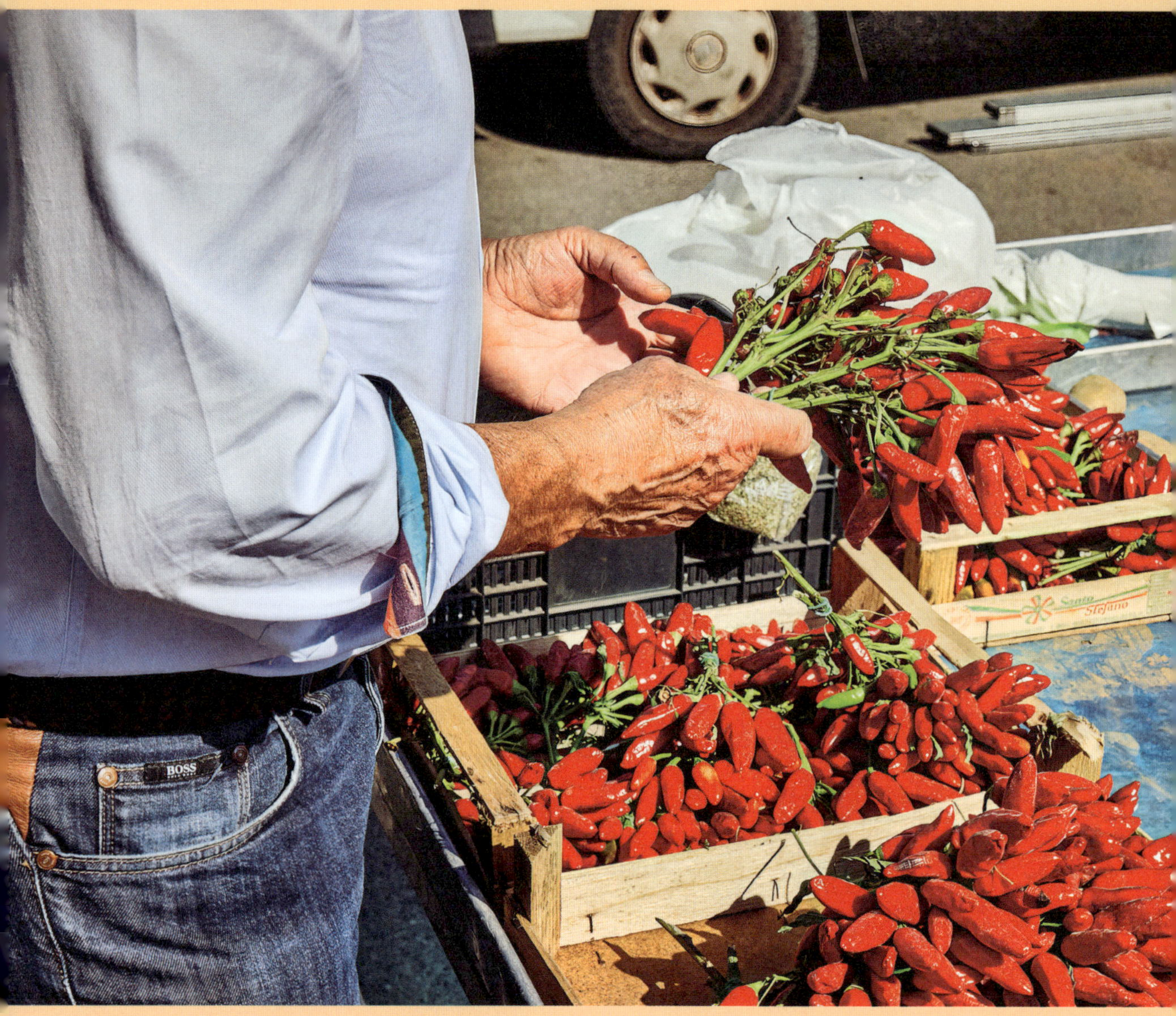

Molise, once a part of Abruzzo until about 50 years ago, is one of the smallest regions of Italy. Its population has been steadily declining over the years due to emigration, but its culture, which feels a little like stepping back in time, is kept very much alive with food festivals that celebrate its local produce – delicious vegetables and pulses, meat and dairy products from the sheep and goats that graze its mountainous terrain, and fish and seafood from its Adriatic coastline. Each summer the locals of the mountainous village of Capracotta celebrate the humble sheep with a delicious mutton stew known as *La Pezzata di Pecora* (see page 198).

In contrast, the most populated region of the South is Campania. The beautiful villages and crystalline waters of its well-known resorts (Sorrento and the Amalfi Coast) mean that it is visited by holidaymakers from all over the globe, and Naples, the region's capital, overlooked by Mount Vesuvius, is a charming mix of chaos and beauty. Campania also boasts a rich history. It was colonized by the Greeks before the Romans, then was invaded by the Normans during the Middle Ages, followed by the French and Spanish, and all these many influences have coloured its customs and cuisine. The nutrient-rich soil of the region ensures excellent produce like aubergines, peppers and the famous sweet Amalfi lemon. It is the home of the San Marzano tomato and buffalo mozzarella and dishes like pizza, spaghetti, caprese salad and clams and mussels, which are the classics of Italian cuisine.

Heading south of Campania is the mountainous region of Basilicata, with its forests and national parks. Also known as Lucania, in the early 20th century it was one of the poorest areas of Italy and, up until the 1970s, many people in the ancient town of Matera lived in squalid conditions in prehistoric grottoes, known as the Sassi. However, these days the cave-like dwellings have been restored and the town is a Unesco World Heritage Site. The cuisine of Basilicata is based on simple, *cucina povera* ingredients like bread, fresh pasta, beans and pulses. Local cured pork products enrich the dishes with flavour to make rich ragùs, as do local cheeses made from cow's and sheep's milk and *peperone crusco* – a speciality made from dried and smoked red peppers. And with such a short coastline, *baccalà* (salt cod) traditionally provides the main supply of fish.

Puglia, the heel of Italy, represents the 'table of Italy'. With its fields of wheat, it has always produced excellent bread, focaccia and pasta, and its age-old olive trees, which dominate the landscape, produce a pungent olive oil that, for me, is liquid gold. Its cuisine is made from good local produce – wonderful cheeses, high-quality beef and lamb for making the richest ragù sauces, and fresh-grown vegetables (peppers, courgettes, beans, tomatoes and greens). Altamura was the first town in Europe to receive a DOP classification for its bread and even the local branch of McDonald's was shunned in favour of local bread and produce and subsequently closed down. Now that is a testament to a region which may not have many Michelin-starred chefs but does produce great, healthy food that everyone can enjoy.

The toe of Italy gives us Calabria, a region still relatively untouched by modern tourism, with an incredibly rich history. The Ancient Greeks settled in Calabria in the 8th century BCE, colonizing much of the coast. The Romans followed, then the Normans, Saracens, Arabs and French. For over 500 years, Albanian communities, fleeing Turkish invasions, took refuge in the region and Calabria is home to a diverse array of dialects – *Grecanico* (Calabrian Greek), *Arabische* (Italo-Albanian) and *Occitan* (a romance language originating from Languedoc in France). And of course, these various nations and communities have influenced not only Calabrian cuisine but many regions of Southern Italy. Calabria's wild landscape, rugged mountains and dramatic coastlines are home to charming old-world towns and villages that are steeped in local traditions. Some of Italy's best potatoes are grown in the Sila Mountains and wild mushrooms can be found there in season. In contrast, hot red chillies and sweet Tropea onions are grown on the fertile lowlands and the former are an indispensable ingredient in *'nduja*, a soft salami which is added to many local dishes (see page 185). Calabria's Adriatic and Mediterranean coastlines bring an array of fish and seafood to the local diet, which also includes preserved fish, like anchovies and sardines.

With its deep history of invaders, coupled with endless hours of sunshine, rugged mountains and never-ending coastlines, Southern Italy really is an eclectic treasure trove of culture and food: from the freshest sun-kissed produce, pungent olive oils, herbs and spices, to a myriad of pasta shapes ready to absorb the rich ragùs and sauces, and the freshest of fish and seafood. Sumptuous desserts and cakes in the pastry shops of Naples aren't to be forgotten, like *Sfogliatelle* or *Polacca Aversana* (see page 214). In my opinion (and I'm biased, of course, as I come from the South) you have not truly visited Italy until you have experienced the southern regions. With its vibrant culture, warmer climate, friendly locals and bold, fresh flavours, there's so much to see in the birthplace of pizza and pasta.

SPAGHETTI ALL'ASSASSINA

Assassin's spaghetti

This unusual way of making spaghetti with tomato dates from the late 1960s, when a chef at a local restaurant in the Puglian city of Bari prepared a dish to satisfy a couple of diners at the end of the night. You can argue that the idea came from the *cucina povera* way of cooking, when leftover pasta was often reheated in a frying pan until a caramelized crust was formed. However, it breaks all the traditions by cooking raw pasta in a very little watery sauce and gradually adding water until it has absorbed, like you would with a risotto. And the result is quite amazing as the flavours of the sauce become absorbed into the pasta.

SERVES 4

300 ml/10 fl oz tomato passata
3 tbsp tomato purée
sea salt
2 litres/3½ pints water
4 tbsp extra virgin olive oil
4 garlic cloves – 2 minced, 2 left whole and lightly crushed
1 red chilli, finely chopped, plus extra slices to garnish
400 g/14 oz spaghetti

In a large saucepan, place the tomato passata and tomato purée with a little salt and top up with 2 litres/3½ pints water. Bring to the boil, then reduce the heat to medium and cook for 10 minutes.

In a large, deep-sided frying pan, place the olive oil over a medium heat and sweat all the garlic and the chilli for a minute to allow it to infuse the oil, then remove the whole cloves and discard them.

Place a couple of ladles of the tomato water in the frying pan, followed by the raw spaghetti. Using tongs or a wooden spoon, press down on the pasta as it cooks so that it caramelizes and forms a crust underneath. After a couple of minutes, turn over to cook the other side in the same way. Add two more ladles of the tomato water and cook the spaghetti over a medium-high heat until the liquid has been absorbed. Add more liquid and keep cooking in this way until the spaghetti is cooked 'al dente'.

Towards the end of the cooking time, cook over a high heat for a couple of minutes to absorb any remaining liquid. Remove the pan from the heat, divide the spaghetti between 4 plates and serve immediately.

MATASSA DI CAPOSELE

Handmade long pasta with chickpeas and dried peppers

This is a very old recipe from the inland towns and villages of the Campania region, where the tradition of making this laborious handmade pasta was lovingly passed down through generations. In Italian, *matassa* means 'a length of loosely-coiled yarn', which is exactly what this pasta shape looks like when it is being made. I'm not sure who makes this pasta at home nowadays, but it can be found in local restaurants in the Avellino and Irpinia areas, often combined with beans or chickpeas and with the addition of dried, long red peppers, *peperoni crusca*, which lend the dish a distinctly smoky flavour.

SERVES 2–4

For the pasta
150 g/5½ oz 00 flour
75 g/2¾ oz durum wheat semolina flour (semola rimacinata)
125 ml/4 fl oz water

For the sauce
2 tbsp extra virgin olive oil
2 dried long red peppers (peperoni crusca)
2 garlic cloves, diced
2 bay leaves
pinch of fennel seeds
1 x 400 g/14 oz tin of chickpeas, plus liqiod
sea salt

First make the pasta. Place both flours in a large bowl or on a clean work surface and mix, then make a well in the centre and gradually add 125 ml/4 fl oz water, mixing to make a soft dough. Knead lightly for about 10 minutes, then form into a ball, cover with a cloth and set aside to rest for at least 30 minutes.

Meanwhile, make the sauce. In a large, deep-sided frying pan, place the olive oil, add the dried peppers and sweat over a medium heat for a couple of minutes to infuse the oil. Remove the peppers and set aside. Add the garlic, bay leaves and fennel seeds to the oil and cook for a minute, ensuring the garlic does not burn. Stir in the chickpeas with their liquid and cook over a medium heat for about 10 minutes until all the flavours are nicely infused. Taste and check for seasoning, adding a little salt if necessary.

Take the ball of dough and, with your hands, make a hole in the centre and gently keep making the hole bigger until you obtain a very long loop. Keep rolling with your hands to get the dough as thin as possible and, to prevent the pasta from drying out, lightly dab your fingers in a little water as you roll the dough (see photos for a better visual explanation!).

Recipe continues overleaf

Bring a large pot of salted water to the boil. Carefully loop the pasta around your hand and drop it into the boiling water. Cook for about 10 minutes until the pasta is nearly 'al dente'.

Using tongs, transfer the pasta, which by now will have broken up, to the chickpea mixture, along with a little of the hot pasta water. Mix well over a medium-high heat for a couple of minutes to finish off cooking the pasta. Crumble in one of the peppers and stir through.

Remove from the heat and serve immediately, garnished with a sprinkling of the remaining crumbled pepper.

Ingredient Note
You can find *peperoni crusca* in good Italian delis or online.

Cooking Note
Although mastering the pasta shape may seem a little daunting at first, it's actually quite easy and fun to make – and if the pasta loop does break in places, don't worry as it will naturally break when immersed in the boiling water anyway.

LAMPASCIONE E PATATE AL FORNO

Roasted lampascioni and potatoes

Lampascioni resemble small onions but are, in fact, bulbs of wild Tassel Hyacinths. Slightly bitter in taste, they have been around since ancient times and are particularly prevalent in the Puglia and Basilicata regions, where they were often consumed among rural communities when times were hard. Over time, they have become quite a delicacy and are now used in all sorts of dishes – focaccia, pastas, fritters – as well as being served alongside roast meat dishes, like in this dish where they combine perfectly with roasted cubed potatoes.

**SERVES 4
(AS A SIDE DISH)**

1 x 280 g/10 oz jar of lampasioni sott'olio (drained weight 180 g/6¼ oz)

300 g/10½ oz potatoes, peeled and cut into small cubes

5 cherry tomatoes, halved

2 garlic cloves, left whole and squashed

½ red chilli, finely sliced

½ handful of flat-leaf parsley, finely chopped

sea salt and freshly ground black pepper

Preheat the oven to 180°C Fan/200°C/400°F/gas mark 6.

Drain the *lampascioni*, reserving the oil.

Place the potatoes in an ovenproof dish or roasting tin together with the *lampascioni*, tomatoes, garlic, chilli and parsley. Season with salt and pepper, pour over the reserved oil and gently stir until thoroughly coated.

Cover with foil and roast in the oven for 45 minutes. After 25 minutes, remove the foil and continue to roast until golden brown. Serve as a side dish.

Ingredient Note
Fresh *lampascioni* are not found outside of Puglia or Basilicata, yet they are often available preserved in oil, so ask your Italian deli or order online.

AFFUNNATIELLA MOLISANA

Green peppers with scrambled eggs

This ancient dish from the small region of Molise in Southern Italy hails from the *cucina povera* and makes use of local ingredients and eggs to bulk up the dish. Sometimes a local sausage is added but my pared-down vegetarian version uses a long pointed green pepper called *friarielli* or *friggitelli,* which should be obtainable from a good greengrocer or international shop. I also opted for scrambled eggs, but you could crack in the eggs with the tomatoes and gently poach them – it makes a delicious brunch.

SERVES 4

8 friarielli peppers (approx. 400 g/14 oz in total)
6 tbsp extra virgin olive oil
1 large onion, finely sliced
340 g/11¾ oz tomatoes, roughly chopped into small pieces
½ handful of basil leaves, roughly torn
8 eggs, lightly beaten
rustic bread, toasted, to serve
sea salt and freshly ground black pepper

With a small sharp knife, carefully slice off the tops of the peppers and remove the seeds and cores.

In a pan, place the whole peppers with 4 tablespoons of olive oil over a medium-high heat, season with a little salt and cook for 5–6 minutes, turning the peppers over until slightly blistered and softened. Remove from the pan and set aside.

In a clean pan, place the remaining olive oil over a low heat, add the onion slices and steam-fry for about 10 minutes until nicely softened – be careful not to burn them.

Increase the heat to medium, stir in the tomatoes and basil and season with salt and pepper, then cook for a couple of minutes until the tomatoes have softened.

Season the eggs with a little salt and pepper, then add to the pan and gently scramble. Place the peppers over the eggs and heat through for about 30 seconds.

Serve immediately with slices of toasted rustic bread.

Ingredient Note
If you can't find *friarielli* peppers, Padrón peppers are a good substitute.

FILEJA CON 'NDUJA E CIPOLLE DI TROPEA

Calabrian fileja pasta with 'nduja and sweet Tropea onions

This handmade Calabrian pasta is similar to the Sicilian *busiate* (see page 74) but smaller, resembling screws. In a lot of southern Italian cooking, pasta is wrapped around a wooden or metal skewer, or when I was a boy an umbrella spoke, to make shapes that are generically known as *pasta al ferretto*. This recipe also incorporates two typically Calabrian ingredients – the sweet, red onion from Tropea, which is so mild and delicious you can eat it raw, and the soft spicy 'nduja salami from the town of Spilinga. I recommend you serve the dish with a glass of cool *Ippolito Pecorello* white wine for a real taste of Calabria.

SERVES 4

400 g/14 oz durum wheat semolina flour (semola rimacinata), plus extra for dusting

200 ml/7 fl oz lukewarm water

For the sauce

4 tbsp extra virgin olive oil

2 Tropea onions, finely sliced

800 ml/28 fl oz tomato passata

a few basil leaves

pinch of sea salt

100 g/3½ oz 'nduja

First make the pasta. Place the flour in a large bowl or on a clean work surface, make a well in the centre and gradually add 200 ml/7 fl oz lukewarm water, mixing to make a soft dough. Knead for 5 minutes until smooth, then form into a ball and rest at room temperature, covered with a cloth, for 45 minutes.

In the meantime, make the sauce. In a frying pan, place the olive oil and onions over a low heat and, covered with a lid, cook for 10 minutes until completely softened. Add the tomato passata along with a little water from rinsing the bottle, and the basil leaves and a pinch of salt, then gently simmer for 15 minutes.

Take small pieces of the dough (each approx. 50 g/1¾ oz) and, on a lightly floured surface, roll into very long, thin, snake-like shapes. Cut into 6 cm/2½ inch lengths, and rub each length between your hands to make them even thinner, then curl them around a thin skewer to resemble screws. Carefully transfer the screws to a lightly floured board and cover with a cloth to avoid the pasta drying out while you make the rest.

Bring a large pot of salted water to the boil and cook the *fileja* for about 20 minutes until cooked.

Near the end of the cooking time, remove the tomato sauce from the heat and crumble in the 'nduja, stirring so it melts.

When the pasta is cooked, use a slotted spoon to transfer it to the pan with the tomato sauce and mix together to combine. Add a little of the pasta water to loosen if necessary, then serve.

POLPETTE DELLA QUARESIMA

Lenten 'meatballs'

When I was a child, we would often have *polpette* (dumplings), made from stale bread and cheese, especially on Fridays and during Lent when meat was forbidden. To me, it's a shame that this dish has declined in popularity over the years, with the preference for minced meat taking centre stage in most meatball recipes, as here, the bread and ricotta make the *polpette* so soft they almost melt in your mouth. This is delicious cooked in a tomato sauce and served with a green side salad for a meat-free meal.

MAKES APPROX. 12

For the polpette

140 g/5 oz stale bread, grated or very finely chopped

40 g/1½ oz grated Parmesan cheese

300 g/10½ oz ricotta, well-drained

2 eggs, lightly beaten

2 garlic cloves, finely chopped

handful of flat-leaf parsley, finely chopped

For the sauce

3 tbsp extra virgin olive oil

2 garlic cloves, left whole and squashed

650 ml/22 fl oz tomato passata

8 basil leaves, plus extra for serving

sea salt and freshly ground black pepper

First make the *polpette*. In a large bowl, combine the bread, Parmesan, ricotta, eggs, garlic and parsley and season with salt and pepper. Using your hands, take pieces of the mixture and roll into balls, roughly the size of golf balls – approx. 40 g/1½ oz each in weight. Set aside.

In a pan (large enough to accommodate the *polpette*), place the olive oil over a medium heat and sweat the garlic cloves for a minute. Add the tomato passata, along with a little water from rinsing the jar or carton, and the basil and season with salt and pepper. Cook until the sauce begins to bubble, then add the *polpette*, cover with a lid and cook over a medium-low heat for 20 minutes, checking from time to time to make sure they don't stick to the bottom of the pan and gently covering them with the tomato sauce.

At the end of the cooking time, increase the heat and cook for a minute or so until the sauce reduces a little.

Remove from the heat and serve with extra basil leaves scattered on top.

TOTANI E PATATE

Stewed squid and potatoes

This Amalfi Coast *cucina povera* classic combines sea and land perfectly. The dish traditionally uses a local variety of squid, known as *totani*, but as this is not available outside of the area, use whatever squid you can find. You can use ready-cleaned calamari rings, or otherwise ask your fishmonger to clean the squid for you. Serve with lots of good, rustic bread and a cool glass of *Greco di Tufo* white wine, as this will immediately transport you to the sensations of the Amalfi Coast.

SERVES 4

2 tbsp extra virgin olive oil
2 garlic cloves, finely chopped
½ red chilli, finely sliced
600 g/1 lb 5 oz cleaned calamari/squid tubes, cut into chunks, keeping the tentacles
4 tbsp white wine
300 g/10½ oz potatoes, peeled and cut into chunks
handful of flat-leaf parsley, finely chopped, plus extra to garnish
100 g/3½ oz cherry tomatoes, halved
rustic bread, to serve
sea salt and freshly ground black pepper

In a large pan, place the olive oil over a medium heat and sweat the garlic and chilli for about 30 seconds, then add the calamari and stir-fry for a minute.

Add the white wine and allow to evaporate slightly. Add the potatoes, parsley and cherry tomatoes and season with salt and pepper. Cover with a lid and cook for 25–30 minutes until the squid and potatoes are cooked through. If, during cooking, the pan becomes too dry, add a little hot water.

Remove the lid, increase the heat and cook over a high heat for about a minute, shaking the pan until you obtain a slightly creamy consistency.

Serve with lots of rustic bread and a sprinkling of extra parsley.

CICERCHIE

Soup of cicerchie

Cicerchie is an ancient pulse and was a popular ingredient in Ancient Egypt and Rome, where it was often ground into flour to make bread. Rich in essential nutrients and vitamins, it was easily grown in Puglia without much intervention, withstanding cold temperatures and dry periods, and made the perfect food for rural families. Resembling chickpeas, but with an earthier taste, it is now making a comeback in Italy and is especially great in soups, such as this one, where half the *cicerchie* is mashed for a lovely, creamy texture. Serve with slices of lightly toasted rustic bread for a nutritious meal.

SERVES 4

400 g/14 oz dried cicerchie, soaked in cold water for at least 12 hours, changing the water a couple of times

2 bay leaves

5 garlic cloves, 2 left whole and squashed, 3 finely chopped

4 tbsp extra virgin olive oil

2 rosemary sprigs

4 sage leaves

90 g/3¼ oz guanciale, very finely chopped

50 g/1¾ oz pancetta, very finely chopped

2 tbsp tomato purée

rustic bread, toasted, to serve

sea salt and freshly ground black pepper

Drain the *cicerchie* and remove the skins – don't worry if you don't remove them all as they come off easily during cooking.

In a large saucepan, place the *cicerchie* with the bay leaves and the 2 whole garlic cloves and cover with fresh water. Bring to the boil, then turn down the heat to medium, skim off any foam and simmer for about 30–40 minutes until cooked through. Drain, reserving the cooking water. Discard the bay leaves and garlic.

In a pan, place the olive oil over a medium heat and sweat the chopped garlic, the rosemary and sage for about a minute. Add the very finely chopped *guanciale* and pancetta and cook for a couple of minutes to render the fat. Stir in the *cicerchie*, season with salt and pepper and cook for a couple of minutes.

Transfer half the contents of the pan to a blender and roughly blend with a couple of tablespoons of the reserved cooking water, then return the mashed mixture to the pan. Mix the tomato purée with a little of the cooking water and add to the pan, together with about 400 ml/14 fl oz of the cooking water. Stir to incorporate and cook for a couple of minutes until heated through.

Serve immediately with slices of lightly toasted rustic bread.

Ingredient Notes
The *cicerchie* needs to soak for at least 12 hours in a couple of changes of water. The *battuto* of guanciale and pancetta provides extra flavour, but make sure you finely chop both cured meats very well before adding them.

POLPETTE NEL CUZZITIELLO

Meatballs 'street food style'

In Naples, anything *cuzzitiello* means it is served and eaten inside a bread roll. Traditionally a *soffritto*, a spicy stew of various animal offal, was served this way as street food and you can find places in Naples where this dish is still made. However, these days meatballs and vegetarian options are more popular and the inspiration for this dish came to me while travelling in Calabria, where I tasted the softest meatballs ever with just a little minced pork for flavour combined with aubergine and softened bread. Using the soft inside of the bread rolls to make the meatballs and serving the dish in the bread cavity means you waste nothing and can enjoy a hearty delicious meal, which I'm sure the kids will love. Of course, if you prefer, you can serve the meatballs on their own or with pasta.

SERVES 4
(MAKES APPROX. 24 MEATBALLS)

1 medium-sized aubergine
1 tbsp extra virgin olive oil
1 garlic clove, finely chopped
150 g/5½ oz minced pork
4 large crusty bread rolls
1 egg
½ handful of flat-leaf parsley, finely chopped
20 g/¾ oz grated Parmesan cheese
plain flour, for dusting
abundant vegetable oil, for shallow frying
sea salt and freshly ground black pepper

For the tomato sauce
2 tbsp extra virgin olive oil
½ small onion, finely chopped
400 ml/14 fl oz tomato passata

Preheat the oven to 200°C Fan/220°C/425°F/gas mark 7.

Prick the aubergine all over with a fork and roast in the hot oven for about 40 minutes until softened, then set aside.

In the meantime, in a pan, place the olive oil over a medium heat and sweat the garlic for a few seconds, then add the minced pork and a little salt and pepper and brown the meat all over. Remove from the heat and transfer the mixture to a bowl, then set aside.

In the same pan, make the tomato sauce. Place the olive oil over a medium heat, add the onion and sweat for a couple of minutes. Add the tomato passata along with a little water from rinsing the jar or carton, partially cover the pan with a lid and cook for about 20 minutes, until thickened. Season, then keep warm over a low heat.

Take the bread rolls, slice a little off the top of each (to form a lid) and scoop out the soft interior – you should have 90 g/3¼ oz of soft bread in total (if you need more, supplement with other bread). Soak the bread in a little water, for a few minutes, until softened. Set aside the hollow bread rolls for later.

Recipe continues overleaf

When the aubergine is cooked, remove from the oven and set aside until cool enough to handle, then discard the skin, squeeze out any excess liquid and finely chop the flesh. Also drain the softened bread, squeezing out any excess water with your hands.

In a bowl, combine the chopped aubergine flesh with the pork, softened bread, egg, parsley and Parmesan. Season with salt and pepper and mix well.

Take small pieces of the mixture and roll into small balls (roughly the size of walnuts), then dust in flour.

Heat abundant vegetable oil in a deep-sided pan and, when hot, add the meatballs a few at a time and cook over a medium-high heat for 2–3 minutes on each side, until golden.

Remove the meatballs using a spider utensil or slotted spoon and drain on kitchen paper to soak up the excess oil, then carefully transfer them to the tomato sauce and cook over a medium heat for a couple of minutes to heat through.

Place a little of the tomato sauce inside each bread roll, then fill with a few meatballs and finish with a little extra tomato sauce.

Serve immediately, each wrapped in a piece of crumpled baking paper or a napkin.

LA PEZZATA DI PECORA

Mutton stew from Molise

In the Molise region, it was traditional for local farmers, twice a year, to move their livestock between their summer and winter pastures. Unfortunately, this practice of *transumanza* (transhumance) is on the decline and yet, each year in August, the rural village of Capracotta holds a *sagra* (food festival) in honour of this custom and celebrates with a boiled mutton stew, expertly cooked in large copper pots for everyone to enjoy. This is my version, which sautés the vegetables and seals the meat to retain flavour. Serve with good rustic bread for mopping up the juices.

SERVES 4–6

1 kg/2 lb 4 oz mutton chunks, boneless
4 tbsp extra virgin olive oil
2 garlic cloves, crushed and sliced in half
1 red chilli, finely chopped
2 small rosemary sprigs
2 onions, finely chopped
2 celery stalks, finely chopped
12 cherry tomatoes, sliced in half
2 large potatoes (approx. 460g/1 lb ¼ oz), peeled and cut into chunks
handful of flat-leaf parsley, finely chopped
sea salt

In a large saucepan, place the mutton, cover with water and cook until foam begins to come to the top. Using a spider utensil, skim as much foam off the surface as possible. Drain the meat and set aside.

In a large pan, place the olive oil over a low heat and sweat the garlic, chilli, rosemary, onions, celery and tomatoes for 1 minute.

Stir in the meat with a little salt and, over a medium-high heat, brown the meat all over. Add enough water to cover the meat and bring to the boil, then reduce the heat, cover with a lid and gently cook for 1½ hours.

Add the potato chunks, increase the heat to medium and continue to cook for 25 minutes until the potato is cooked through but not mushy and most of the liquid has reduced. If it hasn't, remove the lid and cook for about 5 minutes over a high heat.

Sprinkle with the parsley and serve.

Ingredient Note
If you prefer a milder flavour, you can use lamb chunks instead of mutton.

MINESTRA MARITATA

Neapolitan pork and cabbage soup

When I was growing up in Italy, this soup was always a favourite during Eastertime. Made with salt-cured pork and lesser cuts, it was an ongoing celebration of the annual killing of the pig, with the addition of a variety of winter and spring greens. It took a while to make as the pork had to be desalted and, although it may seem quite a fatty type of soup, it really isn't and, as long as the fat is well-skimmed, you obtain a lovely light broth. These days, *Minestra Maritata*, the name of which symbolizes a 'marriage' between meat and vegetables, is not so popular and only a handful of traditional families still make it.

SERVES 6

500 g/1 lb 2 oz salted pork ribs
850 g/1 lb 14 oz pig's trotters, cut into large chunks
175 g/6 oz pig's cheek
90 g/3¼ oz pig's skin
300 g/10½ oz Italian pork sausages
1 large onion, cut into chunks
2 celery stalks, roughly chopped
1 large carrot, roughly chopped
150 g/5½ oz tomatoes, roughly chopped
1 tsp black peppercorns
piece of Parmesan cheese rind
2 vegetable stock pots or cubes
1 small Savoy cabbage (approx. 360 g/12½ oz cleaned weight)
bunch of puntarella (approx. 350 g/12 oz cleaned weight)
200 g/7 oz curly kale, roughly chopped
rustic bread, lightly toasted, to serve

Place the salted pork ribs in cold water and rinse a couple of times, then cover in fresh cold water and leave overnight.

The next day, rinse the pork ribs and place in a large pot along with the other pork pieces and sausages. Cover with fresh cold water, bring to the boil, then skim off the fat and drain.

Transfer all the pork to a clean pot along with the onion, celery, carrot, tomatoes, peppercorns, Parmesan rind and stock pots/cubes, then cover everything with fresh water. Bring to the boil, then lower the heat, partially cover with a lid and gently cook for 1½ hours.

In the meantime, prepare the vegetables; discard the hard outer cabbage leaves and white core and roughly slice the rest. Take the puntarella, remove the outer leaves to reveal the heart and stems and roughly chop the leaves and stems.

Place the prepared greens and the kale in the pot with the pork and continue to cook for about another 30 minutes until the vegetables are cooked.

Remove from the heat and serve with some toasted rustic bread.

U' SARCHIAPONE

Stuffed baked tromboncino

This dish, which uses pumpkins that are long and tubular in shape and known as *tromboncino*, comes from the small seaside village of Atrani on the Amalfi Coast, where it was made for the feast of the patron saint each year in July. Years ago, meat, which was usually too expensive to buy, was added to the filling in honour of Santa Maria Maddalena. These days, the dish has become quite a gourmet delicacy in local restaurants. Serve with a green salad on the side and some good rustic bread to mop up the tomato sauce.

SERVES 4–6

1.2 kg/2 lb 10 oz tromboncino
splash of extra virgin olive oil
150 g/5½ oz minced beef
150 g/5½ oz minced pork
40 g/1½ oz stale bread, soaked in a little milk
3 eggs, 2 lightly beaten
35 g/1¼ oz grated Parmesan cheese
50 g/1¾ oz mozzarella cheese, roughly chopped
½ handful of flat-leaf parsley, finely chopped
4 hard-boiled eggs, cooled and peeled
plain flour, for dusting
abundant vegetable or sunflower oil, for frying
sea salt and freshly ground black pepper
a few basil leaves, to serve

For the tomato sauce
2 tbsp extra virgin olive oil
1 small onion, finely chopped
½ celery stalk, finely chopped
2 x 400 g/14 oz tins of chopped tomatoes
sea salt and freshly ground black pepper

First make the tomato sauce. In a pan, place the olive oil over a medium heat and sweat the onion and celery until softened. Add the tomatoes, season with salt and pepper, then cover with a lid and simmer.

In the meantime, chop the *tromboncino* into 4 pieces and remove the interior flesh to obtain hollow tubes. Peel the skin.

In a small frying pan, heat a splash of olive oil and stir-fry the minced beef and pork to seal. Season to taste, then remove from the heat and set aside to cool.

Preheat the oven to 180°C Fan/200°C/400°F/gas mark 6.

In a bowl, combine the cooked minced meat, softened bread, 1 whole egg, the grated Parmesan, mozzarella, parsley and a little salt and pepper. Use the mixture to stuff the hollow *tromboncino* chunks to halfway, then place a boiled egg inside and continue to stuff with the meat mixture until completely filled.

Dust each *tromboncino* chunk with flour, then dip in beaten egg.

Heat abundant oil in a deep-sided pan and, when hot, add the stuffed *tromboncino* chunks and fry on all sides, until golden brown. Remove and drain on kitchen paper.

Line an ovenproof dish with some of the tomato sauce, place the *tromboncino* chunks on top and pour over the remaining tomato sauce. Cover with foil and bake in the oven for 50 minutes until cooked through.

Remove from the oven, slice and serve.

Ingredient Note

In Neapolitan, *sarchiapone* means someone who is naïve and ridiculous, but why it is linked to this dish, I really don't know. However, if you find *tromboncini* in season, please make this dish as it's really delicious and nutritious.

TORTA TARANTINA

Potato-base pizza

This 'pizza' dough uses potatoes as well as flour and comes from the town of Taranto in Puglia, where this is a common feature of their breadmaking. It is very simple to make as you don't need to leave the dough to rise, and I've added a little grated Parmesan for extra flavour. I also opted for a traditional tomato and mozzarella topping, with a few capers for a lovely salty contrast, but you can, of course, use whatever you like. It's delicious eaten hot or cold.

MAKES 2 X 20-CM/8-INCH PIZZAS

160 g/5¾ oz tinned chopped tomatoes

1 tbsp extra virgin olive oil, plus extra for greasing

180 g/6¼ oz mozzarella cheese, roughly chopped

1 tbsp capers

pinch of dried oregano

For the pizza dough

400 g/14 oz potatoes, peeled and cut into chunks

200 g/7 oz 00 flour, plus extra for dusting

80 g/2¾ oz grated Parmesan cheese

fine, dried breadcrumbs, for dusting

sea salt and freshly ground black pepper

Preheat the oven to 160°C Fan/180°C/350°F/gas mark 4.

First make the dough. Bring a pan of water to the boil and cook the potato chunks until tender and cooked through. Drain well, steam-dry to get all the moisture out, and then mash the potato until smooth. Set aside until it is cool enough to handle.

In a bowl, combine the mashed potato, flour and Parmesan and season with salt and pepper, then mix well until you obtain a dough-type consistency.

Place the dough on a lightly floured work surface and divide into 2 pieces, then shape each piece into a 20-cm/8-inch circle.

Lightly grease a couple of flat baking trays with a little olive oil and lightly dust with fine breadcrumbs, then place the potato pizza bases on top.

In a bowl, combine the tinned tomatoes with the olive oil and season with salt and pepper. Spread this mixture over the potato bases and top with the mozzarella, capers and dried oregano.

Bake in the oven for 25 minutes until the mozzarella has nicely melted and the edges of the dough are golden.

Remove from the oven, set aside to rest for a couple of minutes, then slice and serve.

PITTULE

Savoury fried dough balls

These tasty morsels of fried dough are traditional in Salento, southern Puglia. According to legend, a rural housewife was distracted while making bread, the dough overproved and so she decided to break off small pieces and fry them, and so the *pittule* was born. In the past, they were consumed during many of the annual feasts in honour of the church and its saints. As the recipe has evolved, many different ingredients have been added to enrich the dough and, in this recipe, I have chosen sun-dried tomatoes, olives and capers to represent the delicious flavours of the South.

MAKES APPROX. 16–18

10 g/¼ oz fresh yeast

approx. 120 ml/4 fl oz lukewarm water

280 g/10 oz 00 flour

¾ tsp sea salt

20 g/¾ oz sun-dried tomatoes in oil, drained and very finely chopped

8 pitted olives, very finely chopped

½ tbsp capers, finely chopped

abundant vegetable or sunflower oil, for frying

Dissolve the yeast in a little of the lukewarm water. In a large bowl, combine the flour, salt and yeast mixture, then gradually add approx. 120 ml/4 fl oz lukewarm water, mixing to make a smooth dough. Form into a ball, cover with a cloth and leave to rise in a warm place for 2 hours.

Knead the dough with the sun-dried tomatoes, olives and capers until the flavours are incorporated, then form into a ball, cover with a cloth and leave to rise in a warm place for 1 hour.

Break off small pieces of dough, roughly 30 g/1 oz each, and form into round or oval shapes.

Heat abundant oil in a deep-sided pan and deep-fry the *pittule* in batches for 4–5 minutes until they are golden all over. Remove using a spider utensil or slotted spoon, then drain well on kitchen paper and serve.

Serving Suggestion

Pittule can be eaten in place of bread at mealtimes or they are delicious served with cured meats and cheese as an *aperitivo*, or simply a snack at any time. I love to eat them warm, and you can simply reheat them in the oven to warm through.

PAGNOTTE DI SANTA CHIARA

Tomato and anchovy bread

This filled bread was once made in kitchens all over Naples in honour of Santa Chiara on her feast day. This tradition has now disappeared and it's even rare-to-impossible to find this bread sold in bakeries in Naples. However, they are delicious and, with their simple pizza-like ingredients of dough, tomatoes, anchovies and dried oregano, they have all the hallmarks of simple Neapolitan cooking and are ideal for a packed lunch or to take on a picnic.

MAKES 2 ROUND SMALL-SIZED LOAVES

120 g/4¼ oz potatoes, peeled and cut into chunks
5 g/⅛ oz fresh yeast
approx. 100 ml/3½ fl oz lukewarm water
250 g/9 oz strong white bread flour, plus extra for dusting
¾ tsp sea salt
1½ tbsp extra virgin olive oil

For the filling and topping
2 tbsp extra virgin olive oil
8 anchovy fillets, plus 2 for garnishing
400 g/14 oz cherry tomatoes, halved
1 tsp dried oregano
sea salt

Bring a pan of water to the boil and cook the potato chunks until tender and cooked through. Drain well, steam-dry to get all the moisture out, and then mash the potato. Set aside.

Dilute the yeast in a little of the lukewarm water.

In a bowl, combine the mashed potato, flour, salt, olive oil and yeast mixture, then gradually add enough lukewarm water to form a smooth dough. Knead for about 10 minutes, then form into a ball, cover with a cloth and set aside to rest in a warm place for 2 hours.

Meanwhile, make the filling. In a pan, heat the olive oil and cook the anchovy fillets over a medium heat until they dissolve, then stir in the tomatoes, oregano and some salt and cook over a medium-high heat for 10 minutes until the tomatoes have softened. Remove from the heat and set aside to cool.

Divide the dough into 2 equal-sized pieces and shape each piece into a 20-cm/8-inch circle. Place about a third of the tomato mixture in the middle of each circle, then close up the dough around it like a purse or a large bread roll. Transfer to a lightly floured flat baking tray, cover with a cloth and set aside to rest in a warm place for 45 minutes.

Preheat the oven to 180°C Fan/200°C/400°F/gas mark 6.

Bake the loaves in the oven for 25–30 minutes until golden. Remove from the oven and spread the remaining tomato mixture on top of each loaf, with an anchovy fillet to garnish. Leave to rest for about 5 minutes before serving.

PANE DEL PESCATORE

Fisherman's loaf

As the title suggests, this bread from the Cilentan Coast was made for fishermen when they went out to sea. Once baked, the loaf would be sliced and these slices were dried by the gradually dying wood-fired oven, which created a crispy toast that would last a lot longer than fresh bread. With the addition of anchovies, capers, olives and a few raisins for sweetness, this loaf is delicious but can get quite hard the next day. If you happen to have any left over, cut into slices and double-bake in a very low oven for at least a couple of hours to dry out and crisp up.

MAKES 1 LOAF

9 g/¼ oz fresh yeast

300 ml/10 fl oz lukewarm water

approx. 500 g/1lb 2 oz durum wheat semolina flour (semola rimacinata)

10 g/¼ oz sea salt

6 anchovy fillets, finely chopped

15 g/½ oz capers

45 g/1½ oz pitted olives

10 g/¼ oz raisins

Dissolve the yeast in a little of the lukewarm water. Place the flour and salt in a large bowl or on a clean work surface, make a well in the centre, add the yeast mixture and gradually add 300 ml/10 fl oz lukewarm water, mixing to make a soft dough. Knead for 10 minutes, then form into a ball, cover with a cloth and leave to rise in a warm place for 2 hours.

Take the dough, incorporate the chopped anchovy fillets, the capers, olives and raisins and knead for 10 minutes. Form into a roughly oval shape and make an incision lengthways across the top. Transfer to a baking tray lined with baking paper, cover with a cloth and leave to rest in warm place for 1 hour.

Preheat the oven to 230°C Fan/250°C/480°F/gas mark 9½.

Place the loaf in the oven at this temperature for 5 minutes, then reduce the temperature to 140°C Fan/160°C/325°F/gas mark 3 and continue to bake for 40 minutes until golden.

Remove from the oven and allow to cool a little, then cut into slices and serve.

CHIACCHERE CON SANGUINACCIO FINTO

Carnival pastries with chocolate dip

Chiacchere are delicate fried pastries that are typically made during the Carnival period, almost everywhere in Italy. They are known in different areas by different names, such as *cenci, galani, bugie, frappe* and others. When I was growing up in Southern Italy, we would often enjoy them with a type of chocolate sauce known as *sanguinaccio*. As the name suggests, *sanguinaccio* is pig's blood. Carnival time coincided with the annual killing of the pig in early spring and, as no part of the animal was ever wasted, *sanguinaccio* was combined with sugar and chocolate and a few other ingredients to make a wonderful dessert. As kids, we all knew how it was made and where the main ingredient came from, but we didn't bat an eyelid in those days and filled our bellies with the rich, sweet-tasting treat. Nowadays, the tradition of pig's blood in desserts is no longer permitted and children prefer modern-day chocolate treats! Yet I wanted to recreate my childhood dessert, but this time I have used 'fake' pig's blood chocolate to dip the *chiacchere* in. *Delizioso!*

SERVES 4

For the chiacchere	For the sanguinaccio
250 g/9 oz 00 flour, plus extra for dusting	15 g/½ oz 00 or plain flour, sifted
½ tsp vanilla baking powder (or Paneangeli)	15 g/½ oz cornflour, sifted
25 g/1 oz hard butter, cut into small pieces	100 g/3½ oz caster sugar
35 g/1¼ oz caster sugar	40 g/1½ oz cocoa powder, sifted
2 eggs, lightly beaten	½ tsp ground cinnamon
½ tsp vanilla extract	250 ml/9 fl oz milk
1 tbsp dark rum	1 tsp vanilla extract
abundant vegetable or sunflower oil, for deep-frying	50 g/1¾ oz dark chocolate, roughly chopped
icing sugar, for dusting	1 tbsp dark rum
	10 g/¼ oz butter

Recipe continues overleaf

First make the pastry. In a large bowl, combine the flour and baking powder, add the butter and rub together with your fingertips until the mixture resembles fine breadcrumbs. Stir in the caster sugar, eggs, vanilla extract and rum and work into a smooth dough, kneading well to incorporate all the ingredients. Form into a ball, cover with a cloth and set aside to rest at room temperature for 30 minutes.

Meanwhile, make the chocolate dip. In a small saucepan, combine the flour, cornflour, sugar, cocoa powder and cinnamon. Combine the milk and vanilla extract and then gradually whisk this into the dry ingredients. Place the pan over a low-medium heat, whisking all the time until you obtain a thick consistency.

Remove the pan from the heat and stir in the chocolate, rum and butter, mixing well until nicely melted, then set aside.

Divide the pastry into 4 pieces and, on a lightly floured surface, roll out each piece as thin as you can, into a rectangular shape – or use the no. 3 setting on a pasta machine. Using a pastry cutter, cut out thick ribbons approx. 8–10 cm/3¼–4 inches in length and about 3 cm/1¼ inches wide and then make a small cut in the centre of each as this helps the pastry to puff up while cooking.

Heat abundant oil in a deep-sided pan and, when hot, drop a few *chiacchere* in at a time and fry for a minute or so until golden on all sides. Remove using a spider utensil or slotted spoon and transfer to kitchen paper to drain.

Once the *chiacchere* are all cooked, allow them to cool slightly, then sift over a little icing sugar and serve with the *sanguinaccio* for dipping.

INTORCHIATE ALLE MANDORLE

Almond biscuits

These traditional biscuits from Puglia were originally made for weddings and baptisms. In local dialect, *intorchiate* means 'intertwined', which refers to the shape of the biscuits and is symbolic of the linking of arms between bride and groom or baby and God. They are very simple to make with just a few ingredients. Originally, they were made without butter, but I like to add a little for a slightly richer flavour. Crunchy on the outside but still soft inside, they are a perfect accompaniment to a cup of tea or coffee and can also be enjoyed for breakfast. Stored in an airtight container, they will keep for at least a week.

MAKES APPROX. 22 BISCUITS

275 g/9¾ oz 00 flour, plus extra for dusting

½ tsp baking powder (or Paneangeli)

pinch of sea salt

40 g/1½ oz butter, cut into small pieces

70 g/2½ oz caster sugar, plus extra for dusting

4 tbsp olive oil

5 tbsp white wine (at room temperature)

90 g/3¼ oz whole blanched almonds

In a bowl or stand mixer, combine the flour, baking powder and salt. Add the butter and either rub together with your fingertips until the mixture resembles fine breadcrumbs or, if using a stand mixer, use the flat beater attachment. Stir in the sugar to combine.

In a jug, combine the olive oil and white wine, then gradually add to the bowl or stand mixer, mixing until you obtain a soft dough. Wrap the dough in clingfilm and place in the fridge for 20 minutes to rest.

Preheat the oven to 160°C Fan/180°C/350°F/gas mark 4.

Place the dough on a lightly floured work surface and divide into approx. 22 pieces – each piece weighing 25 g/1 oz. Take each piece and roll between your palms until you have a thin snake-like shape, approx. 25 cm/10 inches in length, then cross over to make a small braid.

Shake a little caster sugar over a plate and lightly dust each braid in it, then place on a baking tray lined with baking paper and top each braid with 3 almonds. Bake in the oven for 20 minutes until golden.

Remove from the oven, transfer to a wire rack and set aside to cool.

POLACCA AVERSANA

Cherry and custard brioche cake

The *Polacca Aversana,* a brioche-based cake with a delicate crème pâtissière and sour cherry filling has, as the title infers, a definite Polish influence and comes from the town of Aversa in Campania. Some say that a Polish nun living in the town's convent gave the recipe to a local baker, while others claim a Polish queen visited the town's convent and was served this for her breakfast. No one knows for sure, but interestingly, there are a few other sweet treats in the Campania region with the flavours of Central Europe, such as the famous *Rum Baba*, which originated in Poland and has since become one of Naples' favourite cakes.

SERVES 6–12

For the dough

140 g/5 oz 0 flour, plus extra for dusting

140 g/5 oz 00 flour

pinch of sea salt

zest of 1 lemon

1 x 7 g/⅛ oz sachet (or 2¼ tsp) of easy-blend dried yeast

50 g/1¾ oz caster sugar

1 egg

100 ml/3½ fl oz milk

50 g/1¾ oz butter, cut into small pieces and softened at room temperature, plus extra for greasing

icing sugar, for dusting

For the filling

500 ml/18 fl oz milk

6 egg yolks

120 g/4¼ oz caster sugar

1 tsp vanilla extract

70 g/2½ oz cornflour

125 g/4½ oz sour cherries in syrup (Amarene cherries), drained

1 small egg yolk beaten with a little milk, for egg wash

First make the cake. In a bowl or stand mixer, combine the flours, salt, lemon zest, dried yeast and sugar. In a jug, lightly beat the egg with the milk, then gradually pour into the flour mixture, alternating with pieces of butter and mixing well together to obtain a smooth, elastic dough. Form into a ball, cover with a cloth and leave to rest in a warm place for 2 hours.

In the meantime, grease a 24-cm/9½-inch round loose-bottomed cake tin or pie dish with some butter and dust with a little flour.

Now prepare the filling. In a saucepan, gently heat the milk but do not boil. Remove from the heat. In a heatproof bowl, whisk the egg yolks, sugar and vanilla extract until pale and creamy, then whisk in the cornflour. Gradually add the warm milk to the bowl, whisking well to avoid any lumps.

Recipe continues overleaf

Transfer the custard mixture to a saucepan, place over a low-medium heat and cook for a couple of minutes, whisking all the time, until thickened. Remove from the heat, pour into a dish and leave to cool.

Preheat the oven to 160°C Fan/180°C/350°F/gas mark 4.

Divide the dough in 2 and roll out each piece into a circle approx. 24 cm/9½ inches in diameter. Line the prepared cake tin or pie dish with one piece, pressing it gently up the sides.

Pour in the custard mixture and arrange the cherries all over, pressing them slightly into the custard.

Cover with the remaining piece of dough, crimping the edges. Brush the top with a little egg wash and then bake in the oven for 25–30 minutes until golden brown.

Leave to rest for about 10 minutes, then carefully remove from the tin and serve with a dusting of sifted icing sugar.

Ingredient Note
You can find jars of *Amarene* (sour cherries in syrup) in international shops and Italian delis.

DOLCETTI DI GALATINA

Sweet treats from Galatina

These unusual sweet treats, which were first mentioned in a recipe book in 1773, come from the town of Galatina in Puglia, where they are also known as *Africani*. They are a little like meringues but use egg yolks instead of whites and, because of this, they were often given to lactating mothers and convalescents. The curious thing about them is that they cook in the residual heat of an oven – you must remember to turn the oven off when they go in! – and they used to be made overnight in bakeries, where they were left to cook in the dying embers of the wood-fired ovens.

MAKES 22

3 egg yolks
100 g/3½ oz caster sugar
1 tsp vanilla extract
zest of ½ lemon

Preheat the oven to 200°C Fan/220°C /425°F/gas mark 7.

In a large bowl, place all the ingredients and, using an electric whisk or stand mixer, whisk together until the sugar has completely dissolved and you have a creamy foamy consistency. If you find the sugar isn't dissolving, add a teaspoon of hot water to speed up the process.

Arrange 22 petit four cases on a flat baking tray and place a teaspoonful of the mixture in each, or you can use a piping bag to do this.

Switch off the oven, then immediately place the *dolcetti* in the oven, shut the door and leave them in there until the oven gets cold.

Storage Note
They are delicious served with a glass of sweet wine, like Marsala, and, kept in an airtight container, they will keep for a couple of weeks.

Ingredient Note
I have added vanilla and lemon zest to mine, but you could add other flavourings, such as finely chopped nuts, if you prefer.

South 219

INDEX

A
Aeolian archipelago 66
affunnatiella molisana 184
Alchermes: sponge, hazelnut cream and marzipan cake 160–2
almonds
  almond and chocolate loaf cake 56
  almond biscuits 58, 212
  almond-filled pastries 118–19
  busiate pasta with Trapani pesto 74
  fruit and honey cake 164–6
amaretti biscuits
  chestnut puddings 62
  courgettes with amaretti 140
anchovies
  filled baked sardines 94
  fisherman's loaf 206
  octopus pie 45–6
  pasta with anchovies and breadcrumbs 72
  seafood couscous 90–2
  sweet and sour chicken liver sauce 147
  tomato and anchovy bread 204
  trout fillets with anchovy sauce 144
  tuna and pickle pie 44
anellini alla pecorara 20–2
aniseed bread 106
apple jam: fruit and honey cake 164–6
apricot jam: filled brioche 158
arrosto di stinco con salsina apicius 50
artichokes 19
assassin's spaghetti 176
aubergines
  frascarelli with vegetable ragù 32–3
  fresh ring pasta with vegetables and ricotta 20–2
  meatballs 'street food style' 194–6
  Sardinian couscous with vegetables 84

B
baci panteschi 110
Basilicata 173
bazotti romagnoli 130
beans
  bean and sausage risotto 152
  handmade pasta with beans 28
  polenta soup 85
  Sardinian couscous with vegetables 84
beef 16, 121, 127
  pasta pie 131–3
  slow-cooked beef 146
  stuffed and boiled chicken 102–3
  stuffed baked tromboncino 200–1
  stuffed beef pot roast 99–100
  three-meat stew 52
biscotti birbi 58
bordatino 85
brandacujin 142
bread 69, 174
  aniseed bread 106
  cheesy cabbage bake 141
  courgettes with amaretti 140
  filled baked sardines 94
  fisherman's loaf 206
  Lenten 'meatballs' 186
  meatballs 'street food style' 194–6
  pasta with anchovies and breadcrumbs 72
  rice bread rolls 155
  Sardinian bread bake with tomato and poached eggs 108
  Sardinian bread rolls filled with potato, cheese and mint 104
  stuffed and boiled chicken 102–3
  stuffed baked tromboncino 200–1
  sweet 'n' savoury ravioli 138
  tomato and anchovy bread 204
brioche 65
  cherry and custard brioche cake 214–16
  filled brioche 158
broad beans: Sardinian couscous with vegetables 84
broccoli: polenta dumplings with sausage and broccoli 48
bruscitti di busto arsizio 146
buchteln 158
budino di castagne 62
buglione toscana di tre carni 52
busiate con pesto trapanese 74

C
cabbage
  as alternative ingredient 34–5
  cheesy cabbage bake 141
  Neapolitan pork and cabbage soup 199
cakes
  almond and chocolate loaf cake 56
  cherry and custard brioche cake 214–16
  fruit and honey cake 164–6
  sponge, hazelnut cream and marzipan cake 160–2
Calabrian fileja pasta with 'nduja and sweet Tropea onions 185
calzoncelli di ceci e cioccolato 60
candied fruit 65
  almond and chocolate loaf cake 56
  fruit and honey cake 164–6
capers
  fisherman's loaf 206
  octopus pie 45–6
  pittule 203
  potato-base pizza 202
  seafood couscous 90–2
  sweet and sour chicken liver sauce 147
  tuna and pickle pie 44
carnival pastries with chocolate dip 208–10
carrots
  cicoria soup with cheese and eggs 42
  fresh ring pasta with vegetables and ricotta 20–2
  Neapolitan pork and cabbage soup 199
  pasta pie 131–3

Sardinian couscous with vegetables 84
  seafood couscous 90–2
  stuffed and boiled chicken 102–3
  three-meat stew 52
casca' di carloforte 84
cassarjelle e fascjule 28
cauliflower: Sardinian couscous with vegetables 84
cavolo nero 15
  as alternative ingredient 42
  bean and sausage risotto 152
  polenta soup 85
cazzarielli con fagioli 28
celery
  cicoria soup with cheese and eggs 42
  fresh ring pasta with vegetables and ricotta 20–2
  mutton stew from Molise 198
  Neapolitan pork and cabbage soup 199
  pasta pie 131–3
  stuffed and boiled chicken 102–3
  stuffed baked tromboncino 200–1
  three-meat stew 52
cheese 69, 121, 127, 173
  baked capelli d'angelo pasta 130
  baked Venetian-style gnocchi 134
  bean and sausage risotto 152
  busiate pasta with Trapani pesto 74
  cheesy cabbage bake 141
  cheesy potato fritters 88
  cicoria soup with cheese and eggs 42
  courgettes with amaretti 140
  flower-shaped ricotta-filled pastries 110
  fresh ring pasta with vegetables and ricotta 20–2
  Lenten 'meatballs' 186
  Neapolitan pork and cabbage soup 199
  pasta pie 131–3
  potato-base pizza 202
  ricotta and cherry tart 54

Sardinian bread bake with tomato and poached eggs 108
Sardinian bread rolls filled with potato, cheese and mint 104
Sardinian malloreddus pasta with sausage and creamy Pecorino 82
savoury spelt bake 40
semolina cubes in meat broth 148
stuffed and boiled chicken 102–3
stuffed baked tromboncino 200–1
stuffed beef pot roast 99–100
walnut lasagne 136–7
cherries
    cherry and custard brioche cake 214–16
    ricotta and cherry tart 54
chestnuts 15
    chestnut puddings 62
chiacchere con sanguinaccio finto 208–10
chichi' 44
chicken
    pasta pie 131–3
    stuffed and boiled chicken 102–3
chickpeas
    chickpea and chocolate pastries 60
    handmade long pasta with chickpeas and dried peppers 178–80
    Sardinian couscous with vegetables 84
chicory: cicoria soup with cheese and eggs 42
chitarra con ragù di agnello 24
chocolate
    almond and chocolate loaf cake 56
    carnival pastries with chocolate dip 208–10
    chestnut puddings 62
    chickpea and chocolate pastries 60
    flower-shaped ricotta-filled pastries 110
    fruit and honey cake 164–6
    sponge, hazelnut cream and marzipan cake 160–2
    watermelon jelly 112

cicerchie soup 192
cicoria cacio e ova 42
cicoria soup with cheese and eggs 42
cime di rape: handmade pasta in a broth of greens and tomato 34–5
cjalsons 138
clams: lorighittas pasta with seafood 78–81
clementines: chickpea and chocolate pastries 60
coffee: chickpea and chocolate pastries 60
coniglio all'ischitana 98
courgettes
    courgettes with amaretti 140
    frascarelli with vegetable ragù 32–3
    fresh ring pasta with vegetables and ricotta 20–2
    mini Milanese fritto misto 150
couscous 65
    couscous Trapanese 90
    Sardinian couscous with vegetables 84
    seafood couscous 90–2
crostata di ricotta e visciole 54
cuscniedd 60
custard
    cherry and custard brioche cake 214–16
    custard-filled pastries 114–15

D
dolce certosino 164–6
dolcetti di galatina 218
duls in brusc 147

E
eggs
    cherry and custard brioche cake 214–16
    cicoria soup with cheese and eggs 42
    green peppers with scrambled eggs 184
    Pope's pasta dish 30
    Sardinian bread bake with tomato and poached eggs 108
    savoury spelt bake 40
    semolina cubes in meat broth 148
    stuffed baked tromboncino 200–1
    sweet treats from Galatina 218

F
falsomagro 99–100
fettuccine alla papalina 30
figs: sweet 'n' savoury ravioli 138
fileja con 'nduja e cipolle di tropea 185
fish 66, 70, 122, 125, 174
    creamy salt cod 142
    filled baked sardines 94
    octopus pie 45–6
    pasta with anchovies and breadcrumbs 72
    seafood couscous 90–2
    sweet and sour chicken liver sauce 147
    tomato and anchovy bread 204
    trout fillets with anchovy sauce 144
    tuna and pickle pie 44
fisherman's loaf 206
flowers: medieval pancakes 38
frascarelli con ragù di verdure 32–3
frittelle di polenta 163
frittelle ubaldine 38
fritto misto, mini Milanese 150
fritto misto moderno alla milanese 150
fruit and honey cake 164–6

G
gathulis 88
gelo di melone 112
genovesi di maria grammatico 114–15
gnocchi alla veneziana 134
guanciale: soup of cicerchie 192

H
ham
    courgettes with amaretti 140
    Pope's pasta dish 30
hazelnut cream: sponge, hazelnut cream and marzipan cake 160–2
honey
    chickpea and chocolate pastries 60
    filled baked sardines 94
    fruit and honey cake 164–6
    honey and walnut pastry roll 59
    honey pie 116
    roast pork shank with Apicius sauce 50
    sponge, hazelnut cream and marzipan cake 160–2

I
ice cream 65
intorchiate alle mandorle 212
Ischia-style rabbit 98
Isole Tremiti 70

J
jam
    filled brioche 158
    fruit and honey cake 164–6
    ricotta and cherry tart 54
jelly, watermelon 112

K
kale
    as alternative ingredient 34–5
    Neapolitan pork and cabbage soup 199

L
la pezzata di pecora 198
la torta salata di gaeta 45–6
lamb 16, 68, 69
    chitarra pasta with lamb ragù 24
    mutton stew from Molise 198
    three-meat stew 52
lampascione e patate al forno 182
lampascioni: roasted lampascioni and potatoes 182
lasagne medievali con le noci 136–7
lemons 66, 173
    cherry and custard brioche cake 214–16
    creamy salt cod 142
    filled brioche 158
    Sardinian couscous with vegetables 84
    sweet and sour chicken liver sauce 147
    sweet polenta fritters 163
    trout fillets with anchovy sauce 144

Lenten 'meatballs' 186
lentils 15
liver
   mini Milanese fritto misto 150
   sweet and sour chicken liver sauce 147
   lorighittas con frutti di mare 78–81

M

malloreddus alla campidanese 82
marzipan 65
   sponge, hazelnut cream and marzipan cake 160–2
matassa di caposele 178–80
meatballs 'street food style' 194–6
medieval pancakes 38
micon ad pan ad ris 155
minestra maritata 199
mint
   medieval pancakes 38
   roast pork shank with Apicius sauce 50
   Sardinian bread rolls filled with potato, cheese and mint 104
mortadella: stuffed beef pot roast 99–100
mushrooms 16
   chitarra pasta with lamb ragù 24
   mini Milanese fritto misto 150
   pasta pie 131–3
mussels: lorighittas pasta with seafood 78–81
mutton 68, 173
   mutton stew from Molise 198

N

'nduja 174
   Calabrian fileja pasta with 'nduja and sweet Tropea onions 185
Neapolitan pork and cabbage soup 199

O

octopus pie 45–6
olives 16, 65, 66, 122
   fisherman's loaf 206
   octopus pie 45–6
   pittule 203
   tuna and pickle pie 44
onions 174
   Calabrian fileja pasta with 'nduja and sweet Tropea onions 185
   chitarra pasta with lamb ragù 24
   cicoria soup with cheese and eggs 42
   frascarelli with vegetable ragù 32–3
   fresh ring pasta with vegetables and ricotta 20–2
   green peppers with scrambled eggs 184
   mutton stew from Molise 198
   Neapolitan pork and cabbage soup 199
   pasta pie 131–3
   polenta soup 85
   Pope's pasta dish 30
   Sardinian bread bake with tomato and poached eggs 108
   Sardinian couscous with vegetables 84
   Sardinian malloreddus pasta with sausage and creamy Pecorino 82
   seafood couscous 90–2
   stuffed and boiled chicken 102–3
   stuffed baked tromboncino 200–1
   three-meat stew 52
   trout fillets with anchovy sauce 144
oranges 65, 66
   almond and chocolate loaf cake 56
   filled baked sardines 94
   honey and walnut pastry roll 59
   honey pie 116

P

pagnotte di santa chiara 204
pan ducale 56
pancakes, medieval 38
pancetta
   bean and sausage risotto 152
   cheesy cabbage bake 141
   cicoria soup with cheese and eggs 42
   handmade pasta with beans 28
   pork rolls 154
   slow-cooked beef 146
   soup of cicerchie 192
pane del pescatore 206
pane frattau 108
pane squarato 106
panini al riso 155
paniscia 152
Parma ham: courgettes with amaretti 140
passata
   assassin's spaghetti 176
   Calabrian fileja pasta with 'nduja and sweet Tropea onions 185
   frascarelli with vegetable ragù 32–3
   handmade pasta with beans 28
   Lenten 'meatballs' 186
   meatballs 'street food style' 194–6
   Sardinian bread bake with tomato and poached eggs 108
   Sardinian malloreddus pasta with sausage and creamy Pecorino 82
pasta 68, 170
   assassin's spaghetti 176
   baked capelli d'angelo pasta 130
   busiate pasta with Trapani pesto 74
   Calabrian fileja pasta with 'nduja and sweet Tropea onions 185
   chitarra pasta with lamb ragù 24
   frascarelli with vegetable ragù 32–3
   fresh ring pasta with vegetables and ricotta 20–2
   handmade long pasta with chickpeas and dried peppers 178–80
   handmade pasta in a broth of greens and tomato 34–5
   handmade pasta with beans 28
   lorighittas pasta with seafood 78–81
   pasta pie 131–3
   pasta with anchovies and breadcrumbs 72
   Pope's pasta dish 30
   Sardinian malloreddus pasta with sausage and creamy Pecorino 82
   sweet 'n' savoury ravioli 138
   walnut lasagne 136–7
pasta all'anciova e muddica 72
pasticcio di pasta alla ferrarese 131–3
peas
   frascarelli with vegetable ragù 32–3
   Pope's pasta dish 30
peppers
   frascarelli with vegetable ragù 32–3
   fresh ring pasta with vegetables and ricotta 20–2
   green peppers with scrambled eggs 184
   handmade long pasta with chickpeas and dried peppers 178–80
pickles: tuna and pickle pie 44
pies
   honey pie 116
   octopus pie 45–6
   pasta pie 131–3
pine kernels
   almond biscuits 58
   chestnut puddings 62
   chickpea and chocolate pastries 60
   filled baked sardines 94
   pasta with anchovies and breadcrumbs 72
pistachios: watermelon jelly 112
pistocchedus prenu 118–19
pittule 203
pizza 170
pizza, potato-base 202
polacca aversana 214–16
polenta 121, 126
   polenta dumplings with sausage and broccoli 48
   polenta soup 85
   sweet polenta fritters 163
polpette della quaresima 186
polpette nel cuzzitiello 194–6
Pope's pasta dish 30
pork 173
   meatballs 'street food style' 194–6
   Neapolitan pork and cabbage soup 199
   pork rolls 154
   roast pork shank with Apicius sauce 50

stuffed and boiled
    chicken 102–3
stuffed baked
    tromboncino 200–1
stuffed beef pot roast
    99–100
three-meat stew 52
potatoes 174
    cheesy potato fritters 88
    creamy salt cod 142
    mutton stew from Molise
        198
    potato-base pizza 202
    roasted lampascioni and
        potatoes 182
    Sardinian bread rolls
        filled with potato,
        cheese and mint 104
    stewed squid and
        potatoes 188
    sweet 'n' savoury ravioli
        138
    tomato and anchovy
        bread 204
prawns
    lorighittas pasta with
        seafood 78–81
    seafood couscous 90–2
pumpkins: stuffed baked
    tromboncino 200–1
puntarella: Neapolitan pork
    and cabbage soup 199

Q
quince jam: fruit and honey
    cake 164–6
quinto quarto 19

R
rabbit 70
    Ischia-style rabbit 98
raisins
    filled baked sardines 94
    fisherman's loaf 206
    sweet 'n' savoury ravioli
        138
    sweet polenta fritters 163
rice 122, 126–7
    bean and sausage risotto
        152
    rice bread rolls 155
ricotta 65
    flower-shaped ricotta-
        filled pastries 110
    fresh ring pasta with
        vegetables and ricotta
        20–2
    Lenten 'meatballs' 186
    ricotta and cherry tart 54
    savoury spelt bake 40

walnut lasagne 136–7
S
sa coccoi prena 104
saffron 16
    chitarra pasta with lamb
        ragù 24
    seafood couscous 90–2
salt cod 19, 173
    creamy salt cod 142
sarde a beccafico 94
sardines: filled baked
    sardines 94
Sardinian bread bake with
    tomato and poached
    eggs 108
Sardinian bread rolls filled
    with potato, cheese and
    mint 104
Sardinian couscous with
    vegetables 84
Sardinian malloreddus pasta
    with sausage and creamy
    Pecorino 82
sausages
    bean and sausage risotto
        152
    Neapolitan pork and
        cabbage soup 199
    pasta pie 131–3
    polenta dumplings with
        sausage and broccoli
        48
    Sardinian malloreddus
        pasta with sausage and
        creamy Pecorino 82
seafood 66, 68, 70, 122,
    125, 174
    lorighittas pasta with
        seafood 78–81
    seafood couscous 90–2
    semolina cubes in meat
        broth 148
seupa a la vapelenentse 141
sfratto di goym 59
shallots
    bean and sausage risotto
        152
    pasta with anchovies and
        breadcrumbs 72
soups
    cicoria soup with cheese
        and eggs 42
    handmade pasta in a
        broth of greens and
        tomato 34–5
    Neapolitan pork and
        cabbage soup 199
    polenta soup 85
    semolina cubes in meat

broth 148
spaghetti all'assassina 176
spelt 15
    savoury spelt bake 40
spinach
    as alternative ingredient
        32–4, 42
    stuffed beef pot roast
        99–100
sponge, hazelnut cream and
    marzipan cake 160–2
squid
    lorighittas pasta with
        seafood 78–81
    seafood couscous 90–2
    stewed squid and
        potatoes 188
su pisteddu di sant'antonio
    116
sultanas: pasta with
    anchovies and
    breadcrumbs 72
surgi sfunnet' co' le foglia
    32–4
suricitti marchigiani 48
sweet and sour chicken liver
    sauce 147
sweet 'n' savoury ravioli 138

T
tarts: ricotta and cherry
    tart 54
tomatoes 170, 173
    busiate pasta with
        Trapani pesto 74
    fresh ring pasta with
        vegetables and ricotta
        20–2
    green peppers with
        scrambled eggs 184
    handmade pasta in a
        broth of greens and
        tomato 34–5
    Ischia-style rabbit 98
    mutton stew from Molise
        198
    Neapolitan pork and
        cabbage soup 199
    octopus pie 45–6
    pittule 203
    potato-base pizza 202
    roasted lampascioni and
        potatoes 182
    stewed squid and
        potatoes 188
    stuffed and boiled
        chicken 102–3
    stuffed baked trombocino
        200–1
    tomato and anchovy

bread 204
torta di farro salata 40
torta polenta e osei 160–2
torta tarantina 202
totani e patate 188
Trentino Aldo-Adige 125
trota comasca 144
trout fillets with anchovy
    sauce 144
tuna 65, 66, 70
    tuna and pickle pie 44
turkey: pasta pie 131–3

U
u cinu pollo ripieno e bollito
    102–3
u' sarchiapone 200–1
uccellini scappati alla
    cremonese 154

W
walnuts
    fruit and honey cake
        164–6
    honey and walnut pastry
        roll 59
    walnut lasagne 136–7
watermelon jelly 112

Z
zucchini all'amaretti 140
zuppa alla valpellinese 141
zuppa imperiale 148

ACKNOWLEDGEMENTS

Thank you to the following for all their help and support in making this book happen:

Liz Przybylski, for writing and research.

Adriana Contaldo, for recipe testing and cooking at the shoots.

David Loftus, for stunning photography.

Libby Silbermann, for beautiful styling and props selection.

Ellen Simmons, for helpful tips and encouragement along the way.

Lily Wilson, for the lovely design.

Laura Russell, Caroline Oestergaard, Alice Kennedy-Owen and Kom Patel from Pavilion for all their hard work.

Citalia Holidays, for help in Calabria during a research trip.

Carmine Porporra (Mino), for help in organizing our shoot in Italy.

And to the following for their help and hospitality while in Italy:

Pasquale Giordano, for delicious cheese.

Michele Apuzzo, for fruit and vegetables.

Pasticceria Gambardella, for cakes and desserts.

Pavilion
An imprint of HarperCollins*Publishers* Ltd
1 London Bridge Street
London SE1 9GF

www.harpercollins.co.uk

HarperCollins*Publishers*
Macken House
39/40 Mayor Street Upper
Dublin 1
D01 C9W8
Ireland

10 9 8 7 6 5 4 3 2 1

First published in Great Britain by Pavilion
An imprint of HarperCollins*Publishers* 2026

Copyright © Pavilion 2026
Text © Gennaro Contaldo 2026

Gennaro Contaldo asserts the moral right to be identified as the author of this work. A catalogue record of this book is available from the British Library.

ISBN 9780008603830

This book contains FSC™ certified paper and other controlled sources to ensure responsible forest management.

For more information visit:
www.harpercollins.co.uk/green

Publishing Director: Laura Russell
Commissioning Editor: Ellen Simmons
Designer: Lily Wilson
Production Controller: Grace O'Byrne
Production Assistant: Emma Hatlen
Photographer: David Loftus
Food Stylist/Prop Stylist: Libby Silbermann
Copyeditor: Vicki Murrell
Proofreader: Anne Sheasby
Indexer: Ruth Ellis
Reproduction: Rival Colour LTD

Printed and bound in China by RR Donnelley APS

All rights reserved. No part of this publication may be reproduced, stored in a retrieval system, or transmitted, in any form or by any means, electronic, mechanical, photocopying, recording or otherwise, without the prior written permission of the publishers.

This book is sold subject to the condition that it shall not, by way of trade or otherwise, be lent, re-sold, hired out or otherwise circulated without the publisher's prior consent in any form of binding or cover other than which it is published and without a similar condition including this condition being imposed on the subsequent purchaser.

WHEN USING KITCHEN APPLIANCES, PLEASE ALWAYS FOLLOW THE MANUFACTURER'S INSTRUCTIONS

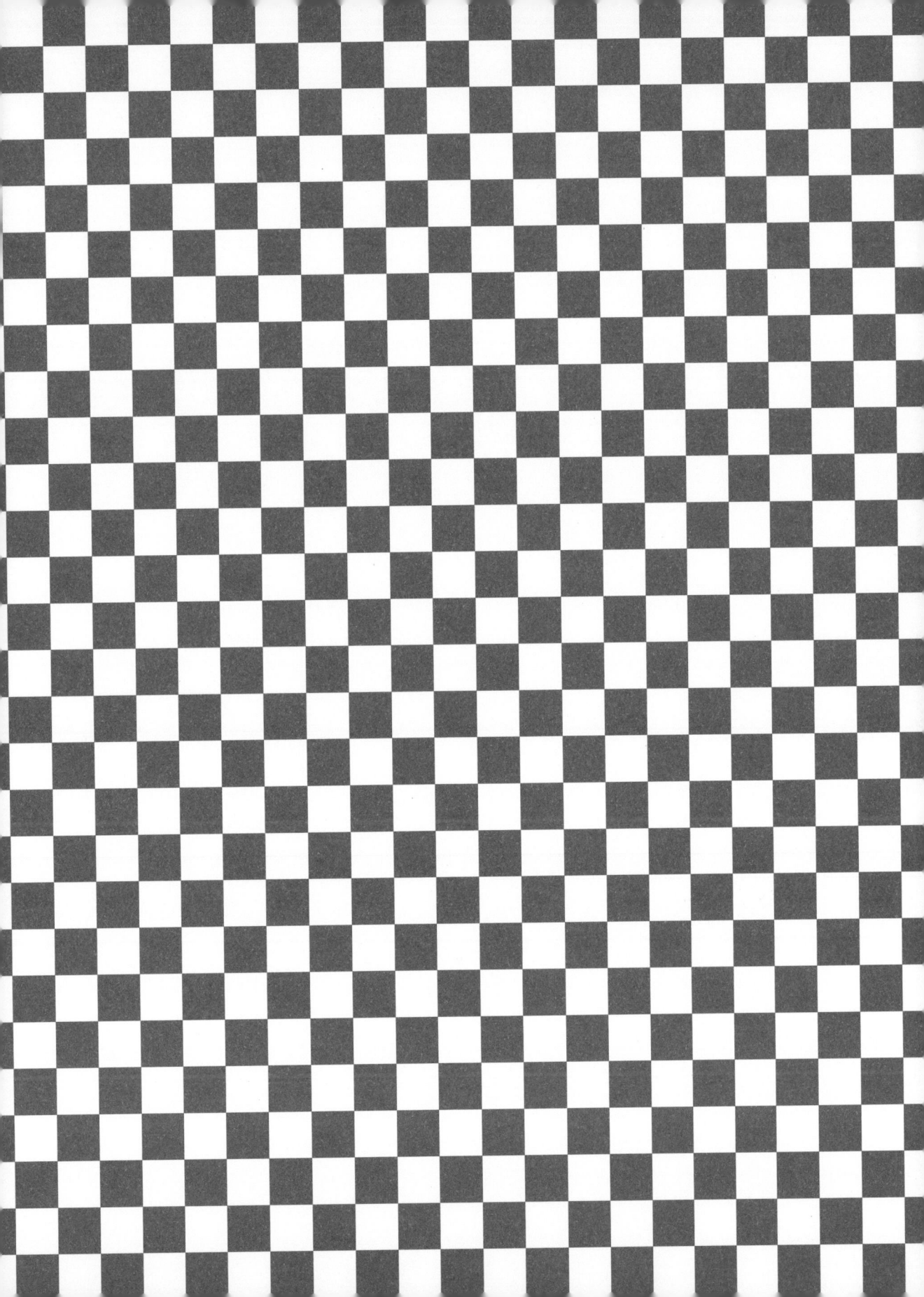

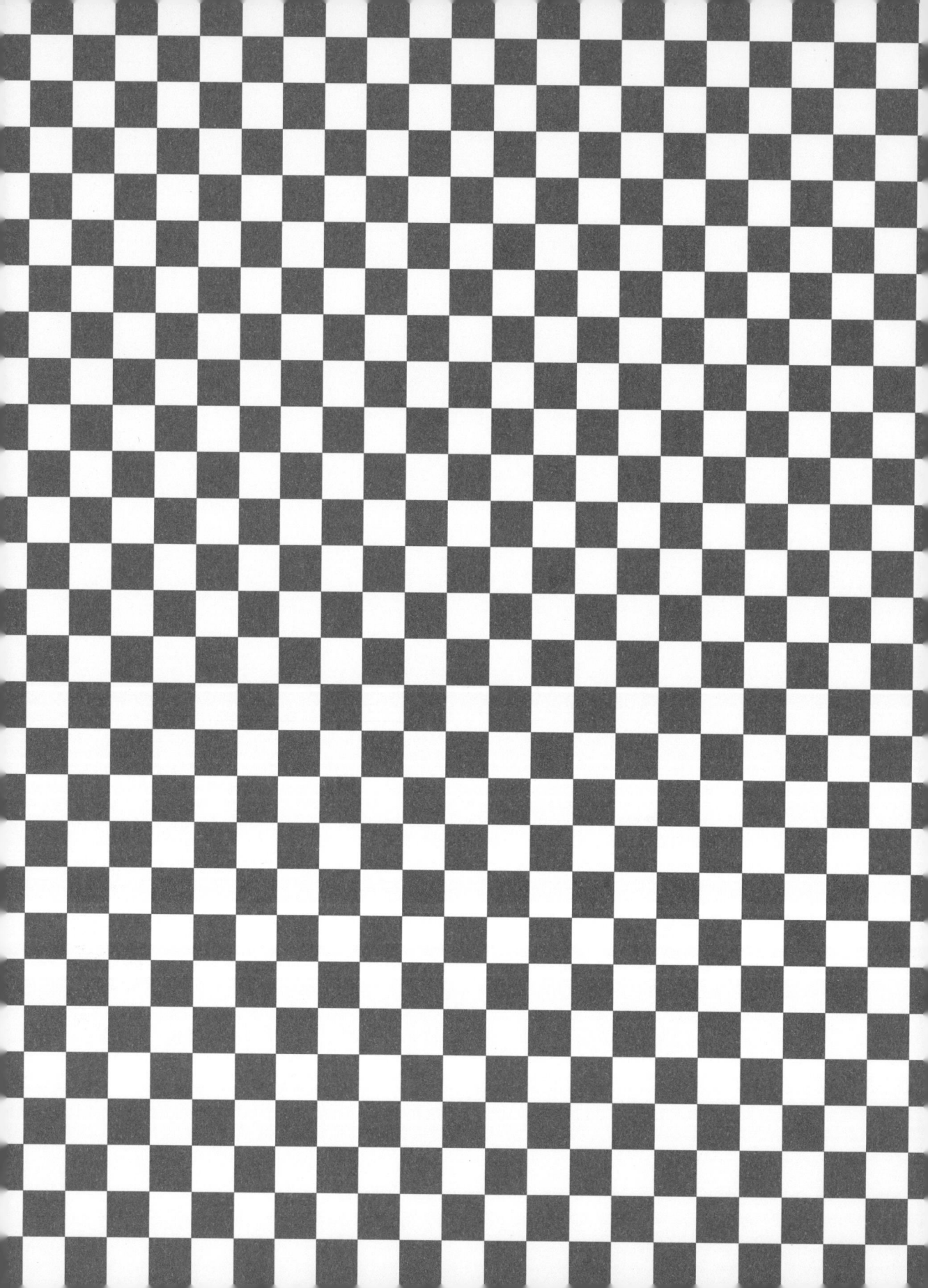